A-Z SLOUGH and WINDSOR

C000254062

CONTENTS

Key to Map Pages   2-3

Map Pages   4-25

Index

REFERENCE

Motorway	**M4**
A Road	A332
B Road	B3022
Dual Carriageway	
One-way Street — Traffic flow on a roads is indicated by a heavy line on the drivers' left.	
Junction Names	LANGLEY ROUNDABOUT
Restricted Access	
Pedestrianized Road	
Track & Footpath	
Residential Walkway	
Railway	Station / Level Crossing / Tunnel
Built-up Area	HIGH ST
Local Authority Boundary	
Posttown Boundary	
Postcode Boundary (within posttown)	
Map Continuation	12

Car Park (selected)	P
Church or Chapel	†
Fire Station	■
Cycleway	
Hospital	H
House Numbers (A & B Roads only)	2 33
Information Centre	i
National Grid Reference	500
Park & Ride — Windsor (Home Park)	P+
Police Station	▲
Post Office	★
Toilet: without facilities for the Disabled	▽
with facilities for the Disabled	▽
Disabled facilities only	▽
Educational Establishment	
Hospital or Hospice	
Industrial Building	
Leisure or Recreational Facility	
Place of Interest	
Public Building	
Shopping Centre or Market	
Other Selected Buildings	

Scale

1:19,000
3⅓ inches (8.47 cm) to 1 mile
5.26 cm to 1 kilometre

0   ¼   ½   ¾ Mile

0   250   500   750 Metres   1 Kilometre

Copyright of Geographers' A-Z Map Company Limited

Fairfield Road, Borough Green, Sevenoaks, Kent TN15 8PP
Telephone: 01732 781000 (Enquiries & Trade Sales)
01732 783422 (Retail Sales)
www.a-zmaps.co.uk

Copyright © Geographers' A-Z Map Co. Ltd.

Ordnance Survey® This product includes mapping data licensed from Ordnance Survey® with the permission of the Controller of Her Majesty's Stationery Office.

© Crown Copyright 2006. All rights reserved. Licence number 100017302

EDITION 5 2007

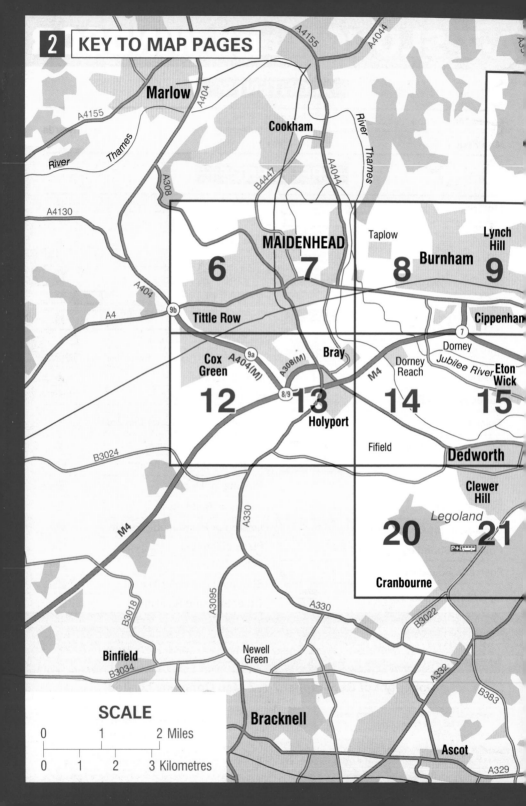

Marlow

Cookham

River Thames

A4155

A404

A4155

A308

A4447

A4044

River Thames

A4130

MAIDENHEAD

Taplow

Lynch Hill

6

7

Burnham

8

9

A404

A4

9b

Tittle Row

Cippenham

7

Dorney

Cox Green

A404(M)

9a

Bray

Dorney Reach

Jubilee River

Eton Wick

12

8/9

13

M4

14

15

Holyport

Dedworth

Fifield

B3024

Clewer Hill

Legoland

M4

A330

20

21

Cranbourne

B3018

B3095

A330

B3022

Binfield

Newell Green

B3034

A332

B383

Bracknell

Ascot

A329

SCALE

0   1   2 Miles

0   1   2   3 Kilometres

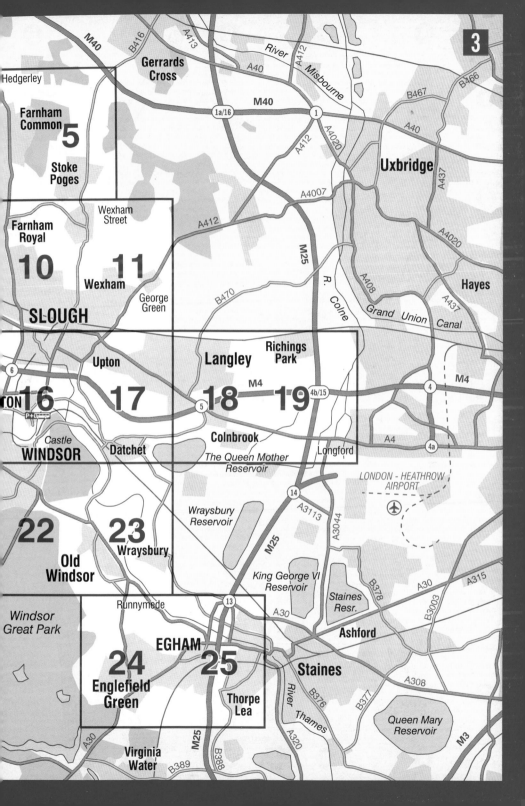

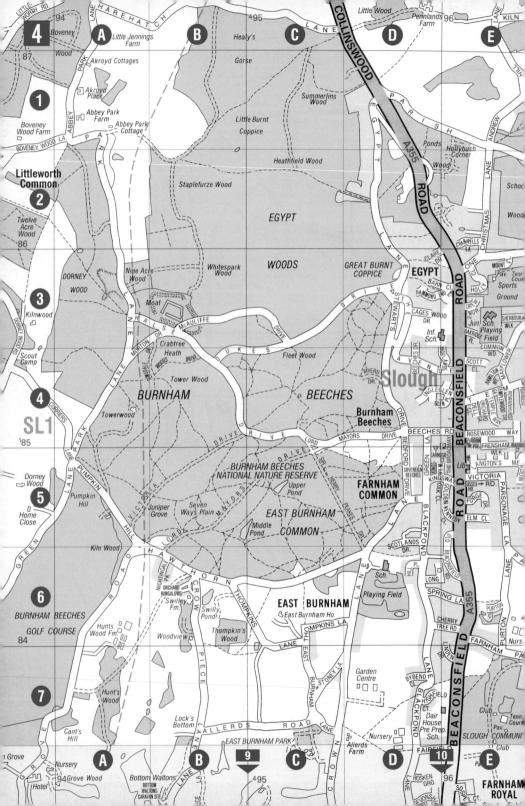

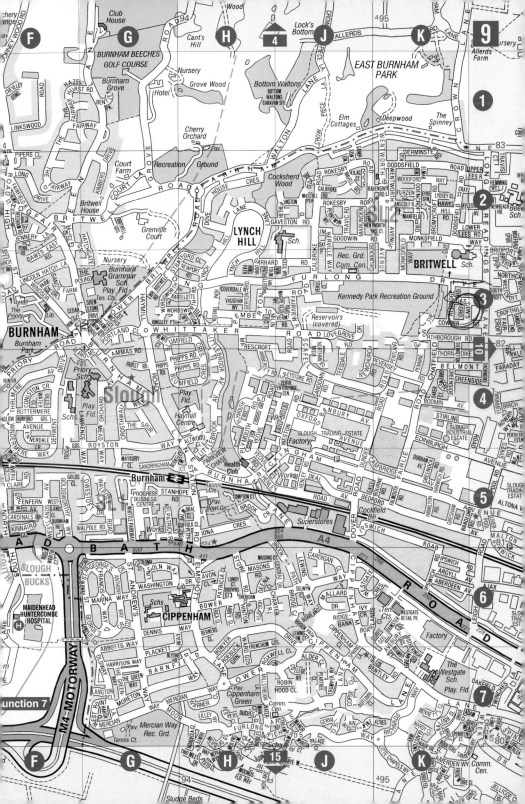

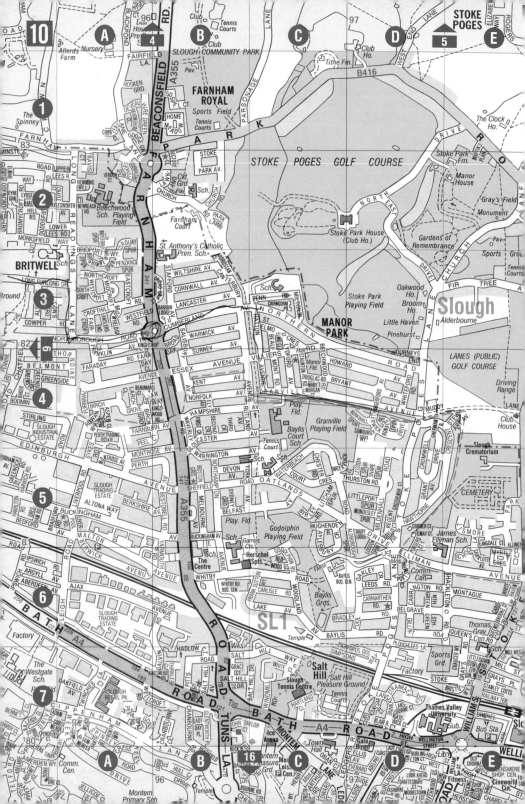

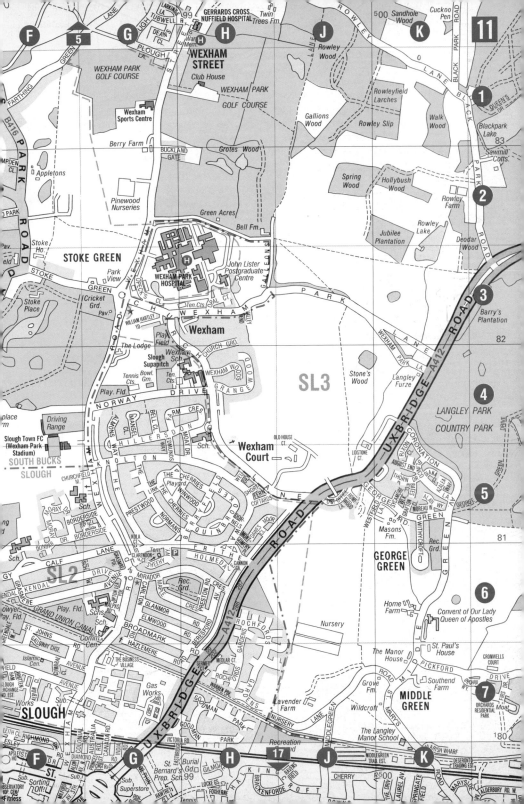

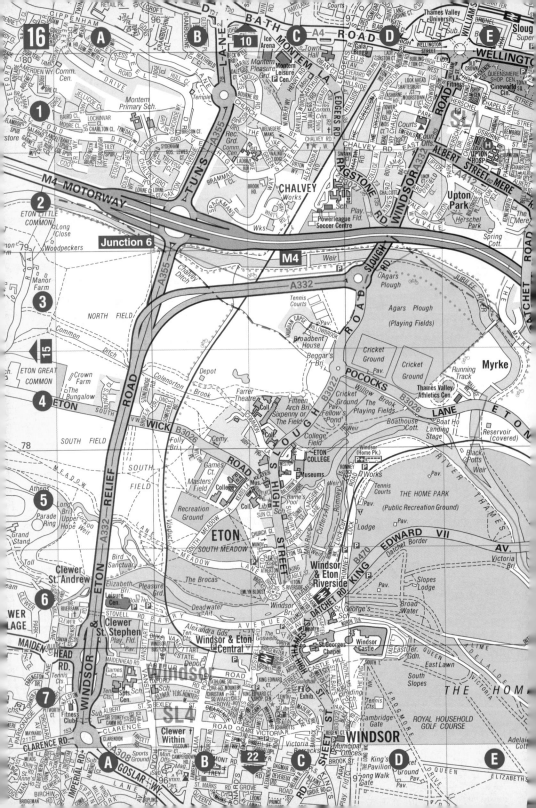

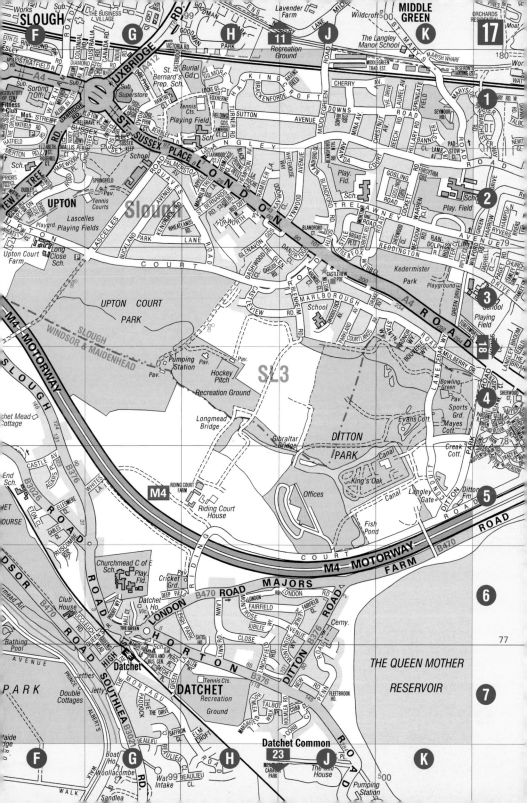

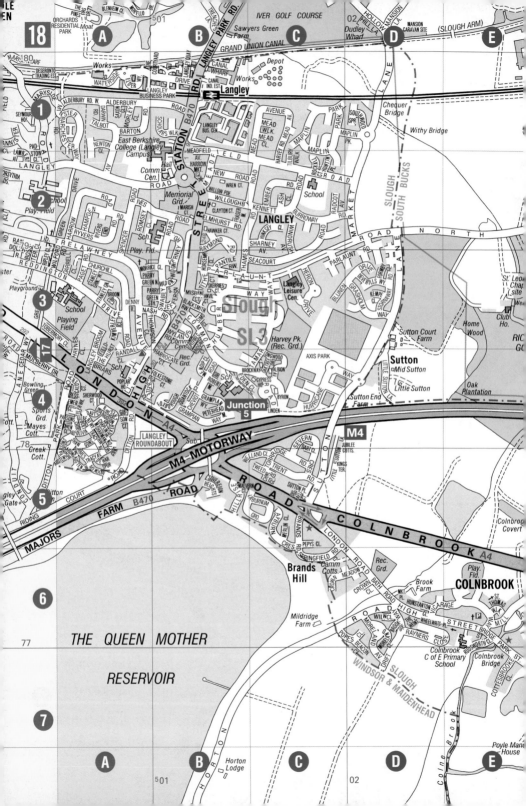

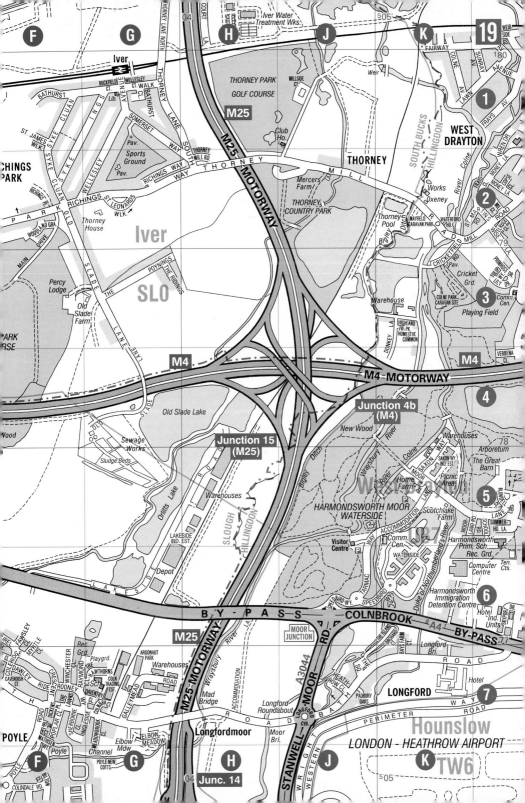

This is a street map (page 23) of the area including Old Windsor, Slough, Wraysbury, Datchet Common, and Runnymede.

Grid reference labels: F, G, H, J (23), K — top row; 1, 2, 3, 4, 5, 6, 7 — right column; F, G, H (24), J, K — bottom row.

23 (top right corner)

THE QUEEN MOTHER RESERVOIR

Slough — SL3

Datchet Common

Mill Place Caravan Park — The Mill House — MILL PL

Pumping Station

Southlea — Southlea Farm — Sandlea Court — Boat Ho — Woollacombe — Water Intake

Monastery Cottages

Welly Farm — DATCHET RD. — HORTON GDS.

THAMES (river)

Albert Bridge — Old Windsor Weir — Nickcroft Ait

Sludge Area — HAM FIELDS — Bird Sanctuary — Sewage Works — Sludge Digestion Lagoons

Sunnymeads — Works — Welley Bri. — Gravel Pit Lake — Nursy — BROOKSIDE AV. — ACACIA AV. — WELLEY AV.

Moram Lodge — Manor Farm

Kingfisher — Bridge Ho — Fairview — HAM LANE — NEW LANE — Ham Bridge — HAM CUT — LANE

Ham Island

Sunnymeads — Gravel Pit Lake — Club — ENGLISH GS. — THE DRIVE — B376 — AVENUE

Library — TAPESTRIES HALL — MANOR FM. COTTS. — Cemy — The Grange — CHURCH CL — POLLARD CL — MEADOW CL — CELL FARM — Church Ho. — The Priory — The Manor — WHITE HERMITAGE — The CL

Old Windsor Lock — Boat Ho — Remenham House — Remenham Park — Hunting Lodge — KINGSWOOD CREEK — KINGSWOOD CREEK — Old Ferry — Old Ferry Ho.

Wraysbury Lake Sailing Club — Gravel Pit Lake — HILL VIEW RD. — THE DRIVE

OLD WINDSOR — ST. LUKE'S RD. — STRAIGHT RD. — BURFIELD — A3021 — B3021

Friary Island — Friary Island — Old Ferry — FRIARY RD — FRIARY

WRAYSBURY — Rec. Grd. — FAIRFIELD — NURSERY WY. — FAIRFIELD WY. — POULCOTT — Sch. — Coach Gr. Ho. — THE GRANGE — Hall — Green Ford — Ten. Cts. — The Green — OLD SCHOOL CT. — HIGH ST. — RD. STA.

Manor Farm Estate

WINDSOR RD. — WELLEY RD. — ST. ANDREWS — HARCOURT RD. — WAYLANDS — MAYLANDS

Staines — TW19

WHARF ROAD — RIVERSIDE — OUSELEY RD — COPPICE DR. — GARSON — LA. RD

Gravel Pit — STAINES — B376 ROAD — WATER CL. — VICARAGE LA.

Dower House — Woodside — Wild Boar Enclosure

PRIEST HILL — WINDSOR ROAD — A308 — A328 — The Lodge — Runnymede House — Priest Hill House — Ten. Cts.

WINDSOR and MAIDENHEAD — RUNNYMEDE — THE EMBANKMENT

Beaumont House — Playing Field — Ten. Cts. — Play. Fld. — Beaumont Farm — Ten. Cts. — Pav.

Runnymede — 24 — RUNNYMEDE ROAD — South Lodge Farm — John F. Kennedy Memorial

Pats Croft Eyot — MEDE RD — MAGNA — CARTA LANE — Magna Carta Island — Ankerwycke Farm — Ankerwycke Priory

500 — **99** — **7.6** — **175** — **94** — **74** — **73** — **68** — **95**

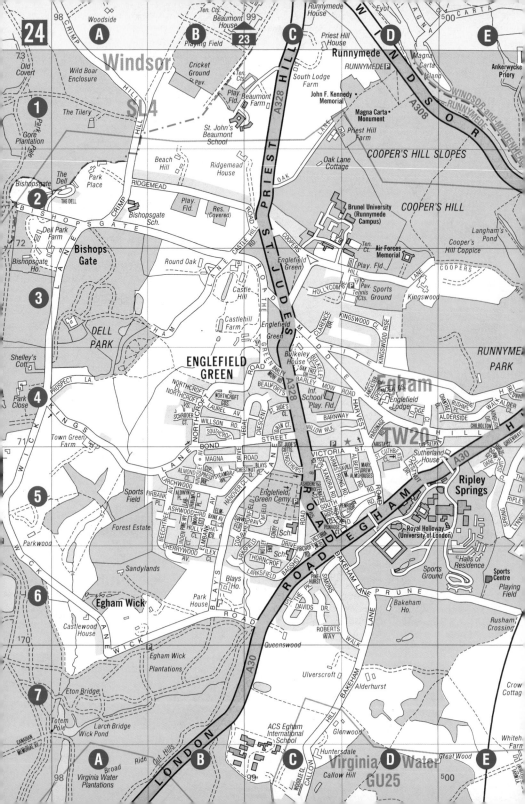

INDEX

Including Streets, Places & Areas, Hospitals & Hospices, Industrial Estates,
Selected Flats & Walkways, Junction Names, Stations and Selected Places of Interest.

HOW TO USE THIS INDEX

1. Each street name is followed by its Postcode District, then by its Locality abbreviation(s) and then by its map reference;
e.g. **Abbey Pk. La.** SL1: Burn . . . .1A **4** is in the SL1 Postcode District and the Burnham Locality and is to be found in square 1A on page **4**. The page number is shown in bold type.

2. A strict alphabetical order is followed in which Av., Rd., St., etc. (though abbreviated) are read in full and as part of the street name;
e.g. **Brook St.** appears after **Brookside Av.** but before **Broom Farm Est.**

3. Streets and a selection of flats and walkways too small to be shown on the maps, appear in the index with the thoroughfare to which it is connected shown in brackets; e.g. **Alexandra Ct.** SL4: Wind . . . .1C **22** (off Alexandra Rd.)

4. Addresses that are in more than one part are referred to as not continuous.

5. Places and areas are shown in the index in BLUE TYPE and the map reference is to the actual map square in which the town centre or area is located and not to the place name shown on the map; e.g. BRAY 1K 13

6. An example of a selected place of interest is Berkshire Yeomanry Mus. 3C 22

7. An example of a station is Burnham Station (Rail) . . . .5G 9. Included are Rail (Rail) and Park & Ride.

8. Junction names are shown in the index in BOLD CAPITAL TYPE; e.g. LANGLEY RDBT. 4B 18

9. An example of a hospital or hospice is GERRARDS CROSS NUFFIELD HOSPITAL 7K 5

GENERAL ABBREVIATIONS

All. : Alley	**Flds.** : Fields	**Pk.** : Park
App. : Approach	**Gdns.** : Gardens	**Pas.** : Passage
Av. : Avenue	**Ga.** : Gate	**Pl.** : Place
Bri. : Bridge	**Gt.** : Great	**Res.** : Residential
Bldgs. : Buildings	**Grn.** : Green	**Ri.** : Rise
Bungs. : Bungalows	**Gro.** : Grove	**Rd.** : Road
Bus. : Business	**Hgts.** : Heights	**Rdbt.** : Roundabout
Cvn. : Caravan	**Ho.** : House	**Shop.** : Shopping
Cen. : Centre	**Ind.** : Industrial	**Sth.** : South
Cir. : Circus	**Info.** : Information	**Sq.** : Square
Cl. : Close	**Junc.** : Junction	**Sta.** : Station
Coll. : College	**La.** : Lane	**St.** : Street
Comn. : Common	**Lit.** : Little	**Ter.** : Terrace
Cnr. : Corner	**Lwr.** : Lower	**Trad.** : Trading
Cotts. : Cottages	**Mnr.** : Manor	**Up.** : Upper
Ct. : Court	**Mans.** : Mansions	**Va.** : Vale
Cres. : Crescent	**Mkt.** : Market	**Vw.** : View
Cft. : Croft	**Mdw.** : Meadow	**Vs.** : Villas
Dr. : Drive	**Mdws.** : Meadows	**Vis.** : Visitors
E. : East	**M.** : Mews	**Wlk.** : Walk
Ent. : Enterprise	**Mus.** : Museum	**W.** : West
Est. : Estate	**Nth.** : North	**Yd.** : Yard
Fld. : Field	**Pde.** : Parade	

LOCALITY ABBREVIATIONS

Bray : **Bray**	Ger X : **Gerrards Cross**	Rich P : **Richings Park**
Burn : **Burnham**	Harm : **Harmondsworth**	Slou : **Slough**
Coln : **Colnbrook**	Hedg : **Hedgerley**	Staines : **Staines**
Dat : **Datchet**	Holy : **Holyport**	Stoke P : **Stoke Poges**
Dor : **Dorney**	Hort : **Horton**	Tap : **Taplow**
Dor R : **Dorney Reach**	Iver : **Iver**	Thorn : **Thorney**
Egh : **Egham**	L'ly : **Langley**	Thorpe : **Thorpe**
Eng G : **Englefield Green**	L Grn : **Littlewick Green**	Vir W : **Virginia Water**
Eton : **Eton**	H'row A : **London Heathrow Airport**	Wat O : **Water Oakley**
Eton W : **Eton Wick**	Lford : **Longford**	W Dray : **West Drayton**
Farn C : **Farnham Common**	Maide : **Maidenhead**	Wex : **Wexham**
Farn R : **Farnham Royal**	Oak G : **Oakley Green**	W Walt : **White Waltham**
Fifi : **Fifield**	Old Win : **Old Windsor**	Wind : **Windsor**
Ful : **Fulmer**	Pal S : **Paley Street**	Wink : **Winkfield**
G Grn : **George Green**	Poyle : **Poyle**	Wray : **Wraysbury**

A

Abbey Cl. SL1: Slou 6H **9**	**Abell Gdns.** SL6: Maide 3C **6**
Abbey Pk. La. SL1: Burn 1A **4**	**Aberdeen Av.** SL1: Slou 6K **9**
Abbots Wlk. SL4: Wind 1H **21**	**Abingdon Wlk.** SL6: Maide 1F **7**
Abbotts Way SL1: Slou 7G **9**	**Acacia Av.** TW19: Wray 3K **23**
	Accommodation La. UB7: Harm 5K **19**
	UB7: Lford 7H **19**
	Acre Pas. SL4: Wind 7C **16**

Adam Cl. SL1: Slou 7K **9**
Addington Cl. SL4: Wind 2K **21**
Addison Ct. SL6: Maide 3J **7**
Adelaide Cl. SL1: Slou 1K **15**
Adelaide Rd. SL4: Wind 7E **16**
Adelaide Sq. SL4: Wind 1C **22**
Adelphi Gdns. SL1: Slou 1D **16**

Adrians Wlk. SL2: Slou . . . 7E **10**
Agars Pl. SL3: Dat . . . 5F **17**
Aintree Cl. SL3: Poyle . . . 7F **19**
Air Forces Memorial . . . 3D **24**
Ajax Av. SL1: Slou . . . 6A **10**
Alan Way SL3: G Grn . . . 5K **11**
Albany Ct. TW20: Egh . . . 3G **25**
Albany Pk. SL3: Coln . . . 7E **18**
Albany Pl. TW20: Egh . . . 3H **25**
Albany Rd. SL4: Old Win . . . 4F **23**
SL4: Wind . . . 1C **22**
Albert Cl. SL1: Slou . . . 2E **16**
Albert Pl. SL4: Eton W . . . 4K **15**
Albert Rd.
SL4: Old Win, Wind . . . 2C **22**
TW20: Eng G . . . 5D **24**
Albert St. SL1: Slou . . . 2E **16**
(not continuous)
SL4: Wind . . . 7A **16**
SL6: Maide . . . 6G **7**
(not continuous)
Albion SL3: L'ly . . . 4C **18**
Albion Cl. SL2: Slou . . . 7F **11**
Albion Pl. SL4: Wind . . . 1K **21**
Aldborough Spur SL1: Slou . . . 5D **10**
Aldbourne Rd. SL1: Burn . . . 4E **8**
Aldebury Rd. SL6: Maide . . . 2F **7**
Alden Vw. SL4: Wind . . . 7G **15**
Alderbury Rd. SL3: L'ly . . . 1A **18**
Alderbury Rd. W. SL3: L'ly . . . 1A **18**
Alder Cl. SL1: Slou . . . 7J **9**
TW20: Eng G . . . 4E **24**
Alderside Wlk. TW20: Eng G . . . 4E **24**
Aldin Av. Nth. SL1: Slou . . . 1F **17**
Aldin Av. Sth. SL1: Slou . . . 1F **17**
Aldridge Rd. SL2: Slou . . . 3K **9**
Aldwick Dr. SL6: Maide . . . 6E **6**
Aldwyn Pl. TW20: Eng G . . . 5B **24**
Alexander Rd. TW20: Egh . . . 4J **25**
(not continuous)
Alexandra Ct. *SL4: Wind . . . 1C 22*
(off Alexandra Rd.)
Alexandra Rd. SL1: Slou . . . 2C **16**
SL4: Wind . . . 1C **22**
SL6: Maide . . . 4E **6**
TW20: Eng G . . . 5C **24**
Alice La. SL1: Burn . . . 3E **8**
Allenby Rd. SL6: Maide . . . 5C **6**
Allen Way SL3: Dat . . . 7H **17**
Allerds Rd. SL2: Farn R . . . 7B **4**
Allington Ct. SL2: Slou . . . 5E **10**
Allkins Ct. SL4: Wind . . . 1C **22**
All Saints Av. SL6: Maide . . . 4D **6**
Alma Ct. SL1: Burn . . . 2F **9**
Alma Rd. SL4: Eton W . . . 3J **15**
SL4: Wind . . . 1B **22**
Almond Cl. SL4: Wind . . . 1A **22**
TW20: Eng G . . . 5B **24**
Almond Rd. SL1: Burn . . . 2F **9**
Almons Way SL2: Slou . . . 4G **11**
Alpha St. Nth. SL1: Slou . . . 1F **17**
Alpha St. Sth. SL1: Slou . . . 2E **16**
Alpha Way TW20: Thorpe . . . 7J **25**
Alpine Cl. SL6: Maide . . . 6H **7**
Alston Gdns. SL6: Maide . . . 5F **7**
Altona Way SL1: Slou . . . 5A **10**
Altwood Bailey SL6: Maide . . . 7C **6**
Altwood Cl. SL1: Slou . . . 4H **9**
SL6: Maide . . . 7C **6**
Altwood Dr. SL6: Maide . . . 7C **6**
Altwood Rd. SL6: Maide . . . 7B **6**
(not continuous)
Alvista Av. SL6: Tap . . . 5E **8**
Alwyn Rd. SL6: Maide . . . 4C **6**
Alyson Ct. SL6: Maide . . . 3G **7**
Amanda Ct. SL3: L'ly . . . 2J **17**
Amberley Ct. SL6: Maide . . . 1K **7**
Amberley Pl. *SL4: Wind . . . 7C 16*
(off Peascod St.)
Amberley Rd. SL2: Slou . . . 4H **9**
Ambleside Way TW20: Egh . . . 6H **25**
Amerden Cl. SL6: Tap . . . 5A **8**
Amerden La. SL6: Tap . . . 5A **8**
(Amerden Cl.)
SL6: Tap . . . 1B **14**
(River Gdns.)
Amerden Way SL1: Slou . . . 1K **15**
Andermans SL4: Wind . . . 7G **15**
Andrew Hill La.
SL2: Hedg . . . 1E **4**
Angelo's *SL4: Eton . . . 4C 16*
(off Common La.)
Ankerwycke Priory . . . 1E **24**
Anne Cl. SL6: Maide . . . 2F **7**
Annie Brookes Cl. TW18: Staines . . . 2K **25**
Ansculf Rd. SL2: Slou . . . 2K **9**
Anslow Pl. SL1: Slou . . . 4F **9**
Anthony Way SL1: Slou . . . 6G **9**
Anvil Ct. SL3: L'ly . . . 3B **18**
Applecroft SL6: Maide . . . 2D **12**
Appletree La. SL3: L'ly . . . 2H **17**
Approach Rd. SL6: Tap . . . 5B **8**
Apsley Ho. SL1: Slou . . . 1F **17**
Arborfield Cl. SL1: Slou . . . 2D **16**
Archer Cl. SL6: Maide . . . 4E **6**
Arches, The *SL4: Wind . . . 7B 16*
(off Goswell Rd.)
Ardrossan Cl. SL2: Slou . . . 3B **10**
Argent Cl. TW20: Egh . . . 5J **25**
Argonaut Pk. SL3: Poyle . . . 7G **19**
Argyll Av. SL1: Slou . . . 6K **9**
Arista Ct. TW20: Eng G . . . 4D **24**
Arkley Ct. SL6: Holy . . . 4K **13**
Arlington Cl. SL6: Maide . . . 4A **6**
Armstrong Rd.
TW20: Eng G . . . 5C **24**
Arndale Way TW20: Egh . . . 4G **25**
Arthur Rd. SL1: Slou . . . 1C **16**
SL4: Wind . . . 7B **16**
Arundel Cl. SL6: Maide . . . 4B **6**
Arundel Ct. SL3: L'ly . . . 3J **17**
Ashbourne Gro. SL6: Maide . . . 2D **12**
Ashbourne Ho. SL1: Slou . . . 1D **16**
Ashbrook Rd. SL4: Old Win . . . 6G **23**
Ash Cl. SL3: L'ly . . . 2C **18**
Ashcroft Ct. SL1: Burn . . . 1E **8**
Ashcroft Rd. SL6: Maide . . . 4D **6**
Ashdene Ho. TW20: Eng G . . . 5C **24**
Ashdown SL6: Maide . . . 1J **7**
Ashenden Wlk. SL2: Farn C . . . 3F **5**
Ashford La. SL4: Dor . . . 1E **14**
Ash Gro. SL2: Stoke P . . . 6H **5**
Ash La. SL4: Wind . . . 1G **21**
Ashleigh Av. TW20: Egh . . . 6J **25**
Ashley Ct. SL6: Maide . . . 5J **7**
Ashley Pk. SL6: Maide . . . 2J **7**
Ashton Pl. SL6: Maide . . . 6B **6**
Ashwood Rd. TW20: Eng G . . . 5B **24**
Aspen Cl. SL2: Slou . . . 4A **10**
Aston Mead SL4: Wind . . . 7H **15**
Astor Cl. SL6: Maide . . . 6J **7**
Atherton Ct. SL4: Eton . . . 6C **16**
Athlone Cl. SL6: Maide . . . 3F **7**
Athlone Sq. SL4: Wind . . . 7B **16**
Atkinson's All. SL6: Maide . . . 4G **7**
Auckland Cl. SL6: Maide . . . 4J **7**
Audley Dr. SL6: Maide . . . 6C **6**
August End SL3: G Grn . . . 5K **11**
Austen Vw. SL3: L'ly . . . 5A **18**
Austen Way SL3: L'ly . . . 5A **18**
Austins Ga. SL6: Maide . . . 4A **6**
Australia Av. SL6: Maide . . . 4G **7**
Australia Rd. SL1: Slou . . . 1G **17**
Autumn Cl. SL1: Slou . . . 7J **9**
Autumn Wlk. SL6: Maide . . . 7B **6**
Avebury SL1: Slou . . . 6K **9**
Avenue, The SL2: Farn C . . . 3D **4**
SL3: Dat . . . 7G **17**
SL4: Old Win . . . 4G **23**
SL6: Maide . . . 2J **7**
TW19: Wray . . . 2J **23**
TW20: Egh . . . 3H **25**
Avenue Rd. SL6: Maide . . . 7J **7**
TW18: Staines . . . 4K **25**
Averil Ct. SL6: Tap . . . 5F **9**
Avon Cl. SL1: Slou . . . 6H **9**
Avondale SL6: Maide . . . 3D **6**
Axis Pk. SL3: L'ly . . . 4C **18**
Ayebridges Av. TW20: Egh . . . 6J **25**
Aylesbury Cres. SL1: Slou . . . 5C **10**
Aylesworth Av. SL2: Slou . . . 2K **9**
Aylesworth Spur
SL4: Old Win . . . 6G **23**
Aysgarth Pk. SL6: Holy . . . 4J **13**
Azalea Way SL3: G Grn . . . 5K **11**

B

Bachelors Acre SL4: Wind . . . 7C **16**
Bader Gdns. SL1: Slou . . . 1K **15**
Badger Cl. SL6: Maide . . . 1E **12**
Badgersbridge Ride SL4: Wink . . . 6E **20**
Badgers Wood SL2: Farn C . . . 4E **4**
Bad Godesberg Way SL6: Maide . . . 5G **7**
Badminton Rd. SL6: Maide . . . 6C **6**
Bagshot Rd. TW20: Eng G . . . 6C **24**
Bailey Cl. SL4: Wind . . . 1K **21**
SL6: Maide . . . 5G **7**
Baird Cl. SL1: Slou . . . 1A **16**
Bakeham La. TW20: Eng G . . . 6D **24**
Bakers La. SL6: Maide . . . 4A **6**
Bakers Row SL6: Maide . . . 4A **6**
Baldwin Pl. SL6: Maide . . . 5D **6**
Baldwin Rd. SL1: Burn . . . 2F **9**
Baldwin's Bec *SL4: Eton . . . 5C 16*
(off Baldwin's Shore)
Baldwins Shore SL4: Eton . . . 5C **16**
Ballard Grn. SL4: Wind . . . 6H **15**
Balmoral SL6: Maide . . . 3C **6**
Balmoral Cl. SL1: Slou . . . 5H **9**
Balmoral Gdns. SL4: Wind . . . 2C **22**
Banbury Av. SL1: Slou . . . 4J **9**
Band La. TW20: Egh . . . 4F **25**
Banks Spur SL1: Slou . . . 1A **16**
Bannard Rd. SL6: Maide . . . 7B **6**
Bannister Cl. SL3: L'ly . . . 1K **17**
Barbicus Ct. SL6: Maide . . . 4J **7**
Barchester Rd. SL3: L'ly . . . 1A **18**
Bardney Cl. SL6: Maide . . . 2E **12**
Bargeman Rd. SL6: Maide . . . 1F **13**
Barley Mead SL6: Maide . . . 7B **6**
Barley Mow Rd. TW20: Eng G . . . 4C **24**
Barn Cl. SL2: Farn C . . . 3D **4**
SL6: Maide . . . 2G **7**
Barn Dr. SL6: Maide . . . 1B **12**
Barnfield SL1: Slou . . . 7G **9**
Barnway TW20: Eng G . . . 4C **24**
Barons Way TW20: Egh . . . 5K **25**
Barrack La. SL4: Wind . . . 7C **16**
Barrow Lodge SL2: Slou . . . 3B **10**
Barr's Rd. SL6: Tap . . . 5E **8**
Barry Av. SL4: Wind . . . 6B **16**
Bartelotts Rd. SL2: Slou . . . 3G **9**
Bartletts La. SL6: Holy . . . 6G **13**
Barton Rd. SL3: L'ly . . . 1A **18**
Basford Way SL4: Wind . . . 2G **21**
Bassett Way SL2: Slou . . . 3H **9**
Bates Cl. SL3: G Grn . . . 5K **11**
Bath Ct. SL6: Maide . . . 6D **6**
Bath Rd. SL1: Slou . . . 6G **9**
SL3: Coln . . . 6D **18**
SL3: Coln, Poyle . . . 7F **19**
SL6: L Grn, Maide . . . 6A **6**
SL6: Tap . . . 5K **7**
UB7: Lford . . . 7J **19**
Bathurst Cl. SL0: Rich P . . . 1G **19**
Bathurst Wlk. SL0: Rich P . . . 1F **19**
Battlemead Cl. SL6: Maide . . . 1K **7**
Baxter Cl. SL1: Slou . . . 2D **16**
Bayley Cres. SL1: Burn . . . 4D **8**
Baylis Bus. Cen. SL1: Slou . . . 6C **10**
Baylis Pde. SL1: Slou . . . 5D **10**
Baylis Rd. SL1: Slou . . . 6C **10**
Bays Farm Ct. UB7: Lford . . . 7K **19**
Bay Tree Ct. SL1: Burn . . . 2F **9**

Beacon Ct. SL3: Coln 6D 18
Beaconsfield Rd.
  SL2: Farn C, Farn R 1B 10
Bears Rails Pk. SL4: Old Win 6E 22
Beaufort Pl. SL6: Bray 1A 14
Beauforts TW20: Eng G 4C 24
Beaulieu Cl. SL3: Dat 7G 17
Beaumaris Ct. SL2: Slou 4A 10
Beaumont Cl. SL6: Maide 2B 12
Beaumont Rd. SL2: Slou 3C 10
  SL4: Wind 1B 22
Beckett Chase SL3: L'ly 4A 18
Beckwell Rd. SL1: Slou 1B 16
Bedford Av. SL1: Slou 5J 9
Bedford Cl. SL6: Maide 2B 12
Bedford Dr. SL2: Farn C 4D 4
Beech Cl. SL6: Maide 4C 6
Beeches Dr. SL2: Farn C 4D 4
Beeches Rd. SL2: Farn C 4D 4
Beechfield Pl. SL6: Maide 1D 12
Beech Rd. SL3: L'ly 1K 17
Beechtree Av. TW20: Eng G 5B 24
Beechwood Dr. SL6: Maide 6B 6
Beechwood Gdns. SL1: Slou 1D 16
Beechwood Rd. SL2: Slou 4C 10
Belfast Av. SL1: Slou 5B 10
Belgrave Pde. SL1: Slou 6D 10
            (off Bradley Rd.)
Belgrave Pl. SL1: Slou 1F 17
Belgrave Rd. SL1: Slou 6D 10
Bell Cl. SL2: Slou 4G 11
Bell La. SL4: Eton W 3J 15
Bell Pde. SL4: Wind 1J 21
Bellsfield Ct. SL4: Eton W 3J 15
            (off Bell La.)
Bells Hill SL2: Stoke P 7J 5
Bells Hill Grn. SL2: Stoke P 6J 5
Bell St. SL6: Maide 6G 7
Bell Vw. SL4: Wind 2J 21
Bell Vw. Cl. SL4: Wind 1J 21
Bell Vue Pl. SL1: Slou 2E 16
Bell Weir Cl. TW19: Staines 1H 25
Belmont SL2: Slou 4K 9
Belmont Cotts. SL3: Coln 6D 18
            (off High St.)
Belmont Cres. SL6: Maide 4D 6
Belmont Dr. SL6: Maide 4E 6
Belmont Pk. Av. SL6: Maide 3E 6
Belmont Pk. Rd. SL6: Maide 4E 6
Belmont Rd. SL6: Maide 4E 6
Belmont Va. SL6: Maide 4E 6
Belvedere Mans. SL1: Slou 1C 16
Bembridge Cl. SL1: Slou 1E 16
Benison Ct. SL1: Slou 2E 16
        (off Hencroft St. Sth.)
Bennetts Cl. SL1: Slou 7K 9
Benning Cl. SL4: Wind 2G 21
Benson Cl. SL2: Slou 7F 11
Bentley Pk. SL1: Burn 1G 9
Bentley Rd. SL1: Slou 7K 9
Beresford Av. SL2: Slou 6H 11
Berkeley Cl. SL6: Maide 4B 6
  TW19: Staines 1K 25
Berkeley Dr. SL4: Wink 7E 20
Berkeley M. SL1: Slou 5G 9
Berkshire Av. SL1: Slou 5A 10
Berkshire Yeomanry Mus. 3C 22
Berners Cl. SL1: Slou 6H 9
Berryfield SL2: Slou 5H 11
Berry Hill SL6: Tap 5A 8
Berwick Av. SL1: Slou 6A 10
Bessemer Cl. SL3: L'ly 4A 18
Bestobell Rd. SL1: Slou 5B 10
Beta Way TW20: Thorpe 7J 25
Bettoney Vere SL6: Bray 1K 13
Beverley Ct. SL1: Slou 1G 17
Beverley Gdns. SL6: Maide 3C 6
Bexley St. SL4: Wind 7B 16
Biddles Cl. SL1: Slou 7H 9
Bideford Spur SL2: Slou 2A 10
Bilton Cl. SL3: Poyle 7F 19
Bingham Pl. SL1: Burn 4D 8

Binghams, The SL6: Bray 2J 13
Birch Gro. SL2: Slou 4A 10
  SL4: Wind 7G 15
Birchington Rd. SL4: Wind 1K 21
Birdwood Rd. SL6: Maide 5B 6
Birley Rd. SL1: Slou 5C 10
Bisham Ct. SL1: Slou 1E 16
            (off Park St.)
Bishop Cen., The SL6: Tap 5C 8
Bishop Ct. SL6: Maide 6E 6
Bishop Ga. SL6: Tap 5C 8
Bishops Farm Cl. SL4: Oak G 1E 20
BISHOPS GATE 2A 24
Bishopsgate Rd. TW20: Eng G 2A 24
Bishops Orchard SL2: Farn R 2A 10
Bishops Rd. SL1: Slou 1F 17
Bishops Way TW20: Egh 5K 25
Bissley Dr. SL6: Maide 2A 12
Bix La. SL6: Maide 3A 6
Blackamoor La. SL6: Maide 3H 7
Blackbird La. SL6: Holy 7H 13
Black Horse Cl. SL4: Wind 1G 21
Black Horse Yd. SL4: Wind 7C 16
Black Lake Cl. TW20: Egh 7G 25
Black Pk. Rd. SL3: Ful, Wex 1K 11
Blackpond La.
  SL2: Farn C, Farn R 5D 4
Blacksmith Row SL3: L'ly 3B 18
Blackthorne Dell SL3: L'ly 2H 17
Blair Rd. SL1: Slou 7D 10
Blakeney Ct. SL6: Maide 3G 7
Blandford Cl. SL3: L'ly 2J 17
Blandford Ct. SL3: L'ly 2J 17
Blandford Rd. Nth. SL3: L'ly 2J 17
Blandford Rd. Sth. SL3: L'ly 2J 17
Blays Cl. TW20: Eng G 5C 24
Blay's La. TW20: Eng G 6B 24
Blenheim Cl. SL3: L'ly 1A 18
Blenheim Ct. TW18: Staines 3K 25
Blenheim Rd. SL3: L'ly 3J 17
  SL6: Maide 4C 6
Blinco La. SL3: G Grn 5C 24
Blind La. SL6: Holy 5J 13
Blondell Cl. UB7: Harm 5K 19
Bloomfield Rd. SL6: Maide 7B 6
Blue Ball La. TW20: Egh 4F 25
Blumfield Ct. SL1: Slou 3G 9
Blumfield Cres. SL1: Slou 3G 9
Blunden Dr. SL3: L'ly 3C 18
Blythe Ho. SL1: Slou 7G 9
Boadicea Cl. SL1: Slou 7H 9
Boarlands Cl. SL1: Slou 6J 9
Boarlands Path SL1: Slou 6J 9
Bodmin Av. SL2: Slou 4K 9
Bold's Ct. SL2: Stoke P 6J 5
Bolton Av. SL4: Wind 2C 22
Bolton Cres. SL4: Wind 2B 22
Bolton Rd. SL4: Wind 2B 22
Bond St. TW20: Eng G 4B 24
Borderside SL2: Slou 5F 11
Borrowdale Cl. TW20: Egh 6H 25
Boscombe Cl. TW20: Egh 7J 25
Boshers Gdns. TW20: Egh 5F 25
Boston Gro. SL1: Slou 5B 10
Bosworth Ct. SL1: Slou 6F 9
Botham Dr. SL1: Slou 2D 16
Bottom Waltons Cvn. Site
  SL2: Farn R 1H 9
Boulters Cl. SL1: Slou 7K 9
  SL6: Maide 3K 7
Boulters Ct. SL6: Maide 3K 7
Boulters Gdns. SL6: Maide 3K 7
Boulters La. SL6: Maide 3K 7
Boulters Lock Island SL6: Maide ..2K 7
Bounce, The SL6: Tap 3B 8
Bourne Av. SL4: Wind 2B 22
Bourne Rd. SL1: Slou 1B 16
Bouverie Way SL3: L'ly 4K 17
BOVENEY 5G 15
Boveney Cl. SL1: Slou 1K 15
Boveney New Rd. SL4: Eton W 3H 15
Boveney Rd. SL4: Dor 3F 15

Boveney Wood La. SL1: Burn 1A 4
Bower Ct. SL1: Slou 6J 9
Bower Way SL1: Slou 6H 9
Bowes Lyon Cl. SL4: Wind 7B 16
            (off Alma Rd.)
Bowes Rd. TW18: Staines 4K 25
Bowmans Cl. SL1: Burn 1E 8
Bowyer Dr. SL1: Slou 7H 9
Boyndon Rd. SL6: Maide 5E 6
BOYN HILL 6E 6
Boyn Hill Av. SL6: Maide 6E 6
Boyn Hill Cl. SL6: Maide 6E 6
Boyn Hill Rd. SL6: Maide 7D 6
Boyn Valley Ind. Est.
  SL6: Maide 6F 7
Boyn Valley Rd. SL6: Maide 7D 6
Bracken Cl. SL2: Farn C 3F 5
Brackenforde SL3: L'ly 1H 17
Bracken Rd. SL6: Maide 1D 12
Bradford Rd. SL1: Slou 5K 9
Bradley Hall TW20: Eng G 2C 24
        (off Coopers Hill La.)
Bradley Rd. SL1: Slou 6C 10
Bradshaw Cl. SL4: Wind 7H 15
Braemar Gdns. SL1: Slou 1K 15
Bramber Ct. SL1: Slou 7K 9
Bramble Dr. SL6: Maide 1B 12
Brambles, The SL6: Holy 5J 13
Bramley Chase SL6: Maide 1D 12
Bramley Cl. SL6: Maide 2D 12
Brammas Cl. SL1: Slou 2B 16
Brampton Ct. SL6: Maide 4J 7
BRANDS HILL 5C 18
Brands Rd. SL3: L'ly 5C 18
BRAY 1K 13
Braybank SL6: Bray 1K 13
Bray Cl. SL6: Bray 2K 13
Bray Ct. SL6: Bray 3K 13
Brayfield Rd. SL6: Bray 1K 13
Bray Rd. SL6: Bray, Maide 6J 7
BRAY WICK 1H 13
Braybank SL6: Bray 1K 13
Braywick Nature Cen. 1H 13
Braywick Rd. SL6: Bray, Maide 6G 7
Braywick Sports Cen. 7H 7
Braywood Av. TW20: Egh 5F 25
Braywood Cotts. SL4: Oak G 1D 20
Breadcroft La. SL6: Maide 2A 12
          (not continuous)
Breadcroft Rd. SL6: Maide 2A 12
Brecon Ct. SL1: Slou 1B 16
Bredward Cl. SL1: Burn 2E 8
Breezes, The SL6: Maide 1F 13
Brewhouse Gallery & Myers Mus.
               ....5C 16
Briar Cl. SL6: Tap 5E 8
Briar Dene SL6: Maide 3D 6
Briars, The SL3: L'ly 4A 18
Briar Way SL2: Slou 4A 10
Brickfield La. SL1: Burn 1D 8
Bridge Av. SL6: Maide 5H 7
Bridge Cl. SL1: Slou 6J 9
  TW18: Staines 3K 25
Bridge Ct. SL6: Tap 5K 7
Bridgeman Ct. SL4: Wind 1K 21
Bridgeman Dr. SL4: Wind 1K 21
Bridge Rd. SL6: Maide 5H 7
Bridge St. SL3: Coln 6E 18
  SL6: Maide 5H 7
Bridgewater Ct. SL3: L'ly 3B 18
Bridgewater Ter. SL4: Wind 7C 16
Bridgewater Way SL4: Wind 7C 16
Bridle Cl. SL6: Maide 3F 7
Bridle Rd. SL6: Maide 3F 7
Bridlington Spur SL1: Slou 2A 16
Bridport Way SL2: Slou 3A 10
Brighton Spur SL2: Slou 3A 10
Brill Cl. SL6: Maide 1E 12
Brinkworth Pl. SL4: Old Win 6G 23
Bristol Way SL1: Slou 7E 10
British Disabled Water-Ski Association
               ....1J 25
BRITWELL 2K 9

Britwell Gdns. SL1: Burn .2G 9
Britwell Rd. SL1: Burn .2F 9
Broadleys SL4: Wind .6J 15
Broadmark Rd. SL2: Slou .6G 11
Broad Oak SL2: Slou .3B 10
Broad Oak Ct. SL2: Slou .3B 10
Broad Platts SL3: L'ly .2J 17
Broadwater Cl. TW19: Wray .6K 23
Broadwater Pk. SL6: Bray .4B 14
Broadway SL4: Wink .7E 20
SL6: Maide .6G 7
Broadway, The SL2: Farn C .5E 4
Brocas St. SL4: Eton .6C 16
Brocas Ter. SL4: Eton .6C 16
Brock La. SL6: Maide .5G 7
Brockton Ct. SL6: Maide .6G 7
Brockway SL3: L'ly .4C 18
Broken Furlong SL4: Eton .4A 16
Brompton Dr. SL6: Maide .3D 6
Bromycroft Rd. SL2: Slou .2K 9
Brook Cres. SL1: Slou .5H 9
Brookdene Cl. SL6: Maide .2G 7
Brook Ho. SL1: Slou .2C 16
Brook Path SL1: Slou .6J 9
(not continuous)
Brookside SL3: Coln .6D 18
Brookside Av. TW19: Wray .2K 23
Brook St. SL4: Wind .1C 22
Broom Farm Est. SL4: Wind .1F 21
Broomfield Ga. SL2: Slou .3A 10
Broom Hill SL2: Stoke P .6J 5
Broom Ho. SL3: L'ly .3A 18
Brownfield Gdns. SL6: Maide .7F 7
Browns Ct. SL1: Slou .6H 9
Bruce Cl. SL1: Slou .7K 9
Bruce Wlk. SL4: Wind .1G 21
Brudenell SL4: Wind .2J 21
Brunel Cl. SL6: Maide .7F 7
Brunel Rd. SL6: Maide .7E 6
Brunel University
Runnymede Campus .2D 24
Brunel Way SL1: Slou .7E 10
Bryant Av. SL2: Slou .4C 10
Bryer Pl. SL4: Wind .2G 21
Buccleuch Rd. SL3: Dat .6F 17
Buckfield Ct. SL0: Rich P .1G 19
Buckingham Av. SL1: Slou .5H 9
Buckingham Av. E. SL1: Slou .5B 10
Buckingham Gdns. SL1: Slou .1E 16
Buckland Av. SL3: Slou .3G 17
Buckland Cres. SL4: Wind .7J 15
Buckland Ga. SL3: Wex .2G 11
Bucklebury Cl. SL6: Holy .4K 13
Buffins SL6: Tap .2B 8
Bulkeley Av. SL4: Wind .2A 22
Bulkeley Cl. TW20: Eng G .4C 24
Bulstrode Pl. SL1: Slou .2E 16
Bunby Rd. SL2: Stoke P .6H 5
Bunce's Cl. SL4: Eton W .4A 16
Bunten Meade SL1: Slou .7A 10
Burcot Gdns. SL6: Maide .1F 7
Burfield Rd. SL4: Old Win .5F 23
Burford Gdns. SL1: Slou .4F 9
Burgett Rd. SL1: Slou .2A 16
Burlington Av. SL1: Slou .1D 16
Burlington Ct. SL1: Slou .1D 16
Burlington Rd. SL1: Burn .3E 8
SL1: Slou .1D 16
Burnetts Rd. SL4: Wind .7H 15
BURNHAM .2F 9
BURNHAM BEECHES .4D 4
Burnham Beeches National Nature Reserve .5B 4
Burnham Cl. SL4: Wind .1G 21
Burnham Hgts. SL1: Slou .5F 9
Burnham La. SL1: Slou .4G 9
Burnham Station (Rail) .5G 9
Burn Wlk. SL1: Burn .2E 8
Burroway Rd. SL3: L'ly .2C 18
Burton Way SL4: Wind .2H 21
Business Village, The SL2: Slou .7G 11
Butlers Cl. SL4: Wind .7G 15
Buttermere Av. SL1: Slou .4F 9
Buttermere Way TW20: Egh .6H 25
Bybend Cl. SL2: Farn R .7D 4
Byland Dr. SL6: Holy .4J 13
Byron SL3: L'ly .4C 18
Byron Ct. SL4: Wind .2K 21
Byways SL1: Burn .4D 8

C

Caddy Cl. TW20: Egh .4G 25
Cadogan Cl. SL6: Holy .5H 13
Cadwell Dr. SL6: Maide .2E 12
Cages Wood Dr. SL2: Farn C .3D 4
Cairngorm Pl. SL2: Slou .3C 10
Calbroke Rd. SL2: Slou .3J 9
Calder Cl. SL6: Maide .3F 7
Calder Ct. SL3: L'ly .4A 18
SL6: Maide .3E 6
Callow Hill GU25: Vir W .7C 24
Cambria Ct. SL3: L'ly .1H 17
TW18: Staines .3K 25
Cambridge Av. SL1: Burn .1E 8
SL1: Slou .5K 9
Cambridge Ho. SL4: Wind .7B 16
Camden Rd. SL6: Maide .3E 6
Camley Gdns. SL6: Maide .4B 6
Camley Pk. Dr. SL6: Maide .4A 6
Camm Av. SL4: Wind .2H 21
Camperdown SL6: Maide .3J 7
Camperdown Ho. SL4: Wind .1B 22
Canada Rd. SL1: Slou .1G 17
Canadian Memorial Av.
TW20: Eng G .7A 24
Canal Ind. Est. SL3: L'ly .1B 18
Canal Wharf SL3: L'ly .1B 18
Cannock Cl. SL6: Maide .6J 7
Cannon Ct. Rd. SL6: Maide .1E 6
(not continuous)
Cannon Ga. SL2: Slou .6H 11
Cannon La. SL6: Maide .6B 6
Canon Hill Cl. SL6: Bray .3K 13
Canon Hill Dr. SL6: Bray .2J 13
Canon Hill Way SL6: Bray .3J 13
Canterbury Av. SL2: Slou .3B 10
Canterbury M. SL4: Wind .1K 21
Cardigan Cl. SL1: Slou .6J 9
Cardinals Wlk. SL6: Tap .5F 9
Carey Cl. SL4: Wind .2A 22
Carisbrooke Cl. SL6: Maide .7D 6
Carisbrooke Ct. SL1: Slou .6E 10
Carlisle Rd. SL1: Slou .6C 10
Carlton Rd. SL2: Slou .6G 11
Carmarthen Rd. SL1: Slou .6D 10
Carnegie Ct. SL2: Farn C .5D 4
Carrington Rd. SL1: Slou .6D 10
Carter Cl. SL4: Wind .1K 21
Castle Av. SL3: Dat .5F 17
Castle Ct. SL6: Maide .5E 6
Castle Dr. SL6: Maide .5E 6
Castle Farm Cvn. Site SL4: Wind .1G 21
Castle Hill SL4: Wind .7C 16
SL6: Maide .5F 7
Castle Hill Rd. TW20: Eng G .3B 24
Castle Hill Ter. SL6: Maide .5F 7
Castle M. SL6: Maide .5F 7
Castle St. SL1: Slou .2E 16
Castleview Pde. SL3: L'ly .3J 17
Castleview Rd. SL3: L'ly .3H 17
Causeway, The SL6: Bray .1J 13
(not continuous)
TW18: Staines .3J 25
Causeway Corporate Cen.
TW18: Staines .3J 25
Cavalry Cres. SL4: Wind .2B 22
Cavendish Cl. SL6: Tap .5D 8
Cavendish Ct. SL3: Poyle .7F 19
Cawcott Dr. SL4: Wind .7H 15
Cecil Way SL2: Slou .3J 9
Cedar Chase SL6: Tap .3A 8
Cedar Cl. SL1: Burn .3F 9
Cedar Ct. SL4: Wind .1K 21
TW20: Egh .3G 25
Cedars, The SL2: Slou .2J 9
Cedars Rd. SL6: Maide .5H 7
Cedar Way SL3: L'ly .4K 17
Cell Farm Av. SL4: Old Win .4G 23
Central Dr. SL1: Slou .6J 9
Central La. SL4: Wink .7E 20
Central Way SL4: Wink .7E 20
Centre, The
Slough .6B 10
Centre Rd. SL4: Wind .6F 15
Century Rd. TW18: Staines .4J 25
Chalcott SL1: Slou .2D 16
Chalgrove Cl. SL6: Maide .6J 7
Challow Ct. SL6: Maide .3E 6
CHALVEY .2C 16
Chalvey Gdns. SL1: Slou .1D 16
Chalvey Gro. SL1: Slou .2A 16
Chalvey Pk. SL1: Slou .1D 16
Chalvey Rd. E. SL1: Slou .1D 16
Chalvey Rd. W. SL1: Slou .1C 16
Chandlers Quay SL6: Maide .5K 7
Chandos Mall *SL1: Slou* *.1E 16*
(off High St.)
Chandos Rd. TW18: Staines .4K 25
Chantry Cl. SL4: Wind .7K 15
Chapel Ct. SL6: Maide .1E 12
Chapel La. SL2: Stoke P .6K 5
Chapels Cl. SL1: Slou .7H 9
Chapel St. SL1: Slou .1E 16
Chaplin M. SL3: L'ly .4A 18
Chapter M. SL4: Wind .6C 16
Chariotts Pl. SL4: Wind .7C 16
Charles Gdns. SL2: Slou .5G 11
Charles Ho. SL4: Wind .7B 16
Charles St. SL4: Wind .7B 16
Charlotte Av. SL2: Slou .6E 10
Charlton SL4: Wind .1F 21
Charlton Cl. SL1: Slou .1A 16
Charlton Pl. *SL4: Wind* *.1F 21*
(off Charlton Way)
Charlton Row SL4: Wind .1F 21
Charlton Sq. *SL4: Wind* *.1F 21*
(off Guards Rd.)
Charlton Wlk. SL4: Wind .1F 21
Charlton Way SL4: Wind .1F 21
Charta Rd. TW20: Egh .4J 25
Charter Cl. SL1: Slou .2E 16
Charter Rd. SL1: Slou .6H 9
Chase, The SL6: Maide .2E 6
Chatfield SL2: Slou .4K 9
Chatham Ct. *SL1: Slou* *.2F 17*
(off Grove Cl.)
Chatsworth Cl. SL6: Maide .7D 6
Chaucer Cl. SL4: Wind .2C 22
Chaucer Way SL1: Slou .7E 10
Chauntry Cl. SL6: Maide .6K 7
Chauntry Rd. SL6: Maide .6J 7
Cheniston Gro. SL6: Maide .5A 6
Cherington Ga. SL6: Maide .3C 6
Cherries, The SL2: Slou .5G 11
Cherry Av. SL3: L'ly .1J 17
Cherry Orchard SL2: Stoke P .6K 5
Cherry Tree Rd. SL2: Farn R .6E 4
Cherrywood Av. TW20: Eng G .6B 24
Chertsey La. TW18: Staines .4K 25
Cherwell Cl. SL3: L'ly .5C 18
SL6: Maide .4H 7
Cheshire Ct. SL1: Slou .1G 17
Chester Rd. SL1: Slou .5C 10
Chestnut Av. SL3: L'ly .1K 17
Chestnut Cl. SL6: Maide .3J 7
TW20: Eng G .5B 24
Chestnut Dr. SL4: Wind .3H 21
TW20: Egh .5D 24
Chestnut Pk. SL6: Bray .3B 14
Cheveley Gdns. SL1: Burn .1F 9
Cheviot Cl. SL6: Maide .6J 7
Cheviot Rd. SL3: L'ly .4B 18
Chichester Ct. SL1: Slou .2G 17
Chilbolton TW20: Egh .4E 24

Chiltern Ct. SL4: Wind 7A 16	Clewer Hill Rd. SL4: Wind 1H 21	Connaught Rd. SL1: Slou 1G 17
(off Fawcett Rd.)	CLEWER NEW TOWN 1A 22	Convent Rd. SL4: Wind 1J 21
Chiltern Ct. M. SL4: Wind 7A 16	Clewer New Town SL4: Wind 1K 21	Conway Rd. SL6: Tap 5E 8
(off Fawcett Rd.)	Clewer Pk. SL4: Wind 6K 15	Cookham Rd. SL6: Maide 2F 7
Chiltern Rd. SL1: Burn 4E 8	CLEWER ST ANDREW 6K 15	Coombe Hill Ct. SL4: Wind 2G 21
SL6: Maide 6J 7	CLEWER ST STEPHEN 6A 16	Coopers Hill La. TW20: Egh, Eng G ..2C 24
Chiltern Rd. SL1: Burn 7B 16	CLEWER VILLAGE 7K 15	(not continuous)
Chilton Ct. SL6: Tap 5F 9	CLEWER WITHIN 7B 16	Cooper Way SL1: Slou 2A 16
Chilwick Rd. SL2: Slou 3J 9	Clifton Cl. SL6: Bray 1H 13	Cope Ct. SL6: Maide 5D 6
Christian Smith Ho. SL6: Maide ...4B 12	Clifton Lodge SL4: Eton W 4K 15	Copper Beech Cl. SL4: Wind 7G 15
Christian Sq. SL4: Wind 7B 16	Clifton Ri. SL4: Wind 7G 15	Copperfield Ter. SL2: Slou 6G 11
Christmas La. SL2: Farn C 2E 4	Clifton Rd. SL1: Slou 1G 17	(off Mirador Cres.)
Church Cl. SL4: Eton 5C 16	Clive Ct. SL1: Slou 1C 16	Coppice Dr. TW19: Wray 6J 23
SL6: Maide 6E 6	Cliveden Mead SL6: Maide 2J 7	Coppice Way SL2: Hedg 1F 5
Church Dr. SL6: Bray 1K 13	Cliveden Rd. SL6: Tap 3A 8	Copse, The SL4: Wink 7D 20
Churchfield M. SL2: Slou 5F 11	Clivemont Rd. SL6: Maide 3G 7	Copse Cl. SL1: Slou 7J 9
Church Gro. SL3: Wex 4H 11	Clockhouse La. E. TW20: Egh 6H 25	UB7: W Dray 2K 19
Church Hill SL6: W Walt 5A 12	Clockhouse La. W. TW20: Egh 6G 25	Copthorn Cl. SL6: Maide 1B 12
Churchill Rd. SL3: L'ly 3A 18	Cloisters, The SL1: Slou 1C 16	Corby Cl. TW20: Eng G 5C 24
CHURCH LAMMAS 3K 25	Clonmel Way SL1: Burn 2E 8	Corby Dr. TW20: Eng G 5B 24
Church La. SL2: Stoke P 3E 10	Close, The SL1: Slou 6G 9	Cordwallis Pk. SL6: Maide 4F 7
SL3: Wex 3G 11	Coachmans Lodge SL4: Wind 1C 22	Cordwallis Rd. SL6: Maide 4F 7
SL4: Wind 7C 16	(off Frances Rd.)	Cordwallis St. SL6: Maide 4F 7
SL6: Bray 1K 13	Coalmans Way SL1: Burn 4D 8	Corfe Gdns. SL1: Slou 6K 9
Church Path SL6: Bray 1K 13	Cobb Cl. SL3: Dat 7J 17	Corfe Pl. SL6: Maide 5D 6
Church Rd. SL2: Farn R 2B 10	Cobblers Cl. SL2: Farn R 1A 10	Cornel Ho. SL4: Wind 2C 22
SL4: Old Win 4G 23	Cobham Cl. SL1: Slou 1J 15	Cornwall Av. SL2: Slou 3B 10
SL6: Maide 7J 7	Cockett Rd. SL3: L'ly 2K 17	Cornwall Cl. SL4: Eton W 4H 15
TW20: Egh 4F 25	Coe Spur SL1: Slou 1A 16	SL6: Maide 2F 7
Church St. SL1: Burn 3F 9	Coftards SL2: Slou 5H 11	Cornwell Rd. SL4: Old Win 5F 23
SL1: Slou 1B 16	Colenorton Cres. SL4: Eton W 3H 15	Coronation Av. SL3: G Grn 4K 11
(Damson Gro.)	Coleridge Cres. SL3: Poyle 7F 19	SL4: Wind 1F 23
SL1: Slou 1E 16	Colin Way SL1: Slou 2A 16	Cotswold Cl. SL1: Slou 2B 16
(Osborne St.)	College Av. SL1: Slou 2D 16	SL6: Maide 6J 7
SL4: Wind 7C 16	SL6: Maide 5F 7	Cottage Pk. Rd. SL2: Hedg 1F 5
TW18: Staines 3K 25	TW20: Egh 5H 25	Cottesbrooke Cl. SL3: Coln 7E 18
Church Ter. SL4: Wind 1H 21	College Cres. SL4: Wind 1A 22	Cotton Hall Ho. SL4: Eton 5B 16
Church Vw. SL6: W Walt 5A 12	College Glen SL6: Maide 5E 6	(off Eton Wick Rd.)
Church Views SL6: Maide 4G 7	College Ri. SL6: Maide 5E 6	Coulson Way SL1: Burn 4E 8
Church Wlk. SL1: Burn 3E 8	College Rd. SL1: Slou 7J 9	Court Cl. SL6: Bray 3K 13
(not continuous)	SL6: Maide 4E 6	Court Cres. SL1: Slou 5C 10
Church Wood Reserve 1G 5	Colley Hill La. SL2: Hedg 2H 5	Court Dr. SL6: Maide 1K 7
Churchyard, The SL6: Bray 1K 13	Collier Cl. SL6: Maide 3G 7	Court Farm Ho. SL1: Slou 7A 10
Cineworld Cinema	Collinswood Rd. SL2: Farn C 1C 4	Courtfield Dr. SL6: Maide 6D 6
Slough 1E 16	Collum Grn. Rd.	Courthouse Rd. SL6: Maide 5D 6
Cinnamon Cl. SL4: Wind 7J 15	SL2: Farn C, Hedg, Stoke P 2F 5	Courtlands SL6: Maide 6G 7
CIPPENHAM 6H 9	COLNBROOK 6E 18	Courtlands Av. SL3: L'ly 3J 17
Cippenham Cl. SL1: Slou 6J 9	Colnbrook By-Pass SL3: Coln, L'ly ..5D 18	Court La. SL0: Iver 1H 19
Cippenham La. SL1: Slou 6J 9	UB7: Harm 6J 19	(not continuous)
Clandon Av. TW20: Egh 6J 25	Colnbrook Cl. SL3: Poyle 7G 19	SL1: Burn 2G 9
Clappers Mdw. SL6: Maide 3J 7	Coln Cl. SL6: Maide 4G 7	SL4: Dor 2D 14
Clare Dr. SL2: Farn C 3D 4	Colndale Rd. SL3: Poyle 7F 19	Court Rd. SL6: Maide 2K 7
Clarefield Cl. SL6: Maide 3B 6	Colne Av. UB7: W Dray 1K 19	Courtyard, The SL3: L'ly 1B 18
Clarefield Dr. SL6: Maide 3B 6	Colne Pk. Cvn. Site UB7: W Dray ...3K 19	Coverdale Way SL2: Slou 3H 9
Clarefield Rd. SL6: Maide 3C 6	Colne Way TW19: Staines 1H 25	Cowper Rd. SL2: Slou 3K 9
Clare Gdns. TW20: Egh 4G 25	Coln Trad. Est. SL3: Poyle 7G 19	COX GREEN 2C 12
Claremont Rd. SL4: Wind 1B 22	Colonial Rd. SL1: Slou 1F 17	Cox Grn. La. SL6: Maide 2C 12
TW18: Staines 4K 25	Colonnade SL6: Maide 5H 7	Cox Grn. Rd. SL6: Maide 1D 12
Clarence Ct. SL4: Wind 7A 16	Combermere Cl. SL4: Wind 1A 22	Crabtree Office Village
TW20: Egh 4F 25	Common, The UB7: W Dray 3K 19	TW20: Thorpe 7J 25
(off Clarence St.)	Common La. SL4: Eton 4C 16	Crabtree Rd. TW20: Thorpe 7J 25
Clarence Cres. SL4: Wind 7B 16	Common La. Ho. SL4: Eton 4C 16	CRANBOURNE 7E 20
Clarence Dr. TW20: Eng G 3C 24	(off Common La.)	Cranbourne Av. SL4: Wind 1J 21
Clarence Rd. SL4: Wind 1K 21	Common Rd. SL3: L'ly 3B 18	Cranbourne Cl. SL1: Slou 7B 10
Clarence St. TW20: Egh 5F 25	SL4: Dor, Eton W 3F 15	Cranbourne Hall Cvn. Site
Clarendon Copse SL6: Maide 6E 6	SL4: Eton W 4J 15	SL4: Wink 7D 20
Clarendon Ct. SL2: Slou 6G 11	Common Wood SL2: Farn C 3E 4	Cranbourne Hall Cotts. SL4: Wink ..7E 20
SL4: Wind 7A 16	Compton Cl. SL1: Slou 5H 9	Cranbourne Rd. SL1: Slou 7B 10
Clare Rd. SL6: Maide 6E 6	Compton Dr. SL6: Maide 4B 6	Cranbrook Dr. SL6: Maide 3C 6
SL6: Tap 5F 9	Concorde Ct. SL4: Wind 1K 21	Cranwells La. SL2: Farn C 2E 4
Clayhall La. SL4: Old Win 4E 22	Concorde Rd. SL6: Maide 1E 12	Craufurd Ct. SL6: Maide 4F 7
(not continuous)	Concorde Way SL1: Slou 1B 16	Craufurd Ri. SL6: Maide 4F 7
Clayton Ct. SL3: L'ly 2B 18	Conduit La. SL3: L'ly 5K 17	Crayle St. SL2: Slou 2K 9
Cleares Pasture SL1: Burn 2E 8	Conegar Ct. SL1: Slou 7D 10	Creden Cl. SL6: Maide 3E 6
Clements Cl. SL1: Slou 1G 17	Conifer La. TW20: Egh 4J 25	Crescent, The SL1: Slou 1D 16
Clevehurst Cl. SL2: Stoke P 5J 5	Conifers, The SL6: Maide 4B 6	(not continuous)
Cleveland Cl. SL6: Maide 6J 7	Conifer Wlk. SL4: Wind 6F 15	SL6: Maide 5F 7
Cleves Ct. SL4: Wind 2J 21	Coningsby Cl. SL6: Maide 2E 12	TW20: Egh 5E 24
Clewer Av. SL4: Wind 1K 21	Coningsby La. SL6: Fifi 7K 13	Crescent Dale SL6: Maide 6G 7
Clewer Ct. Rd. SL4: Wind 6A 16	Coniston Cres. SL1: Slou 4F 9	Crescent Dr. SL6: Maide 5F 7
Clewer Flds. SL4: Wind 7B 16	Coniston Way TW20: Egh 6H 25	Cress Rd. SL1: Slou 1A 16
CLEWER GREEN 1J 21	Connaught Cl. SL6: Maide 3F 7	Cresswells Mead SL6: Holy 4J 13
CLEWER HILL 2H 21		

Cricketfield Rd. UB7: W Dray 3K **19**
Crimp Hill SL4: Eng G, Old Win 6E **22**
TW20: Eng G 2A **24**
Crispin Way SL2: Farn C 3F **5**
Croft, The SL6: Maide 7D **6**
Croft Cnr. SL4: Old Win 4G **23**
Crofters SL4: Old Win 5F **23**
Crofthill Rd. SL2: Slou 3A **10**
Cromer Ct. SL1: Slou 5D **10**
Cromwell Dr. SL1: Slou 5D **10**
Cromwell Rd. SL6: Maide 5E **6**
Cromwells Ct. SL3: L'ly 7K **11**
Cross Oak SL4: Wind 1K **21**
Crossways TW20: Egh 5K **25**
Crossways Ct. *SL4: Wind* *1B* ***22***
(off Osbourne Rd.)
Crosthwaite Way SL1: Slou 4G **9**
Crouch La. SL4: Wink 6B **20**
Crown Cl. SL3: Coln 6D **18**
Crown Cotts. SL4: Wind 3C **22**
Crown La. SL2: Farn R 1K **9**
SL6: Maide 5H **7**
Crown Mdw. SL3: Coln 6C **18**
Crown St. TW20: Egh 3G **25**
Crow Piece La. SL2: Farn R 6B **4**
(not continuous)
Croxley Ri. SL6: Maide 6E **6**
Crummock Cl. SL1: Slou 5F **9**
Culham Dr. SL6: Maide 2F **7**
Cullerns Pas. SL6: Maide 6G **7**
Culley Way SL6: Maide 1B **12**
Cumberland Av. SL2: Slou 3B **10**
Cumberland St. TW18: Staines 4K **25**
Cumbrae Cl. SL2: Slou 7F **11**
Cumbria Cl. SL6: Maide 1D **12**
Curfew Yd. SL4: Wind 6C **16**
Curls La. SL6: Maide 1F **13**
Curls Rd. SL6: Maide 1E **12**
Curriers La. SL1: Burn 4A **4**
Curzon Mall *SL1: Slou* *1E* ***16***
(off Wellington St.)
Cut, The SL2: Slou 3K **9**
Cypress Ho. SL3: L'ly 4C **18**
Cypress Wlk. TW20: Eng G 5B **24**

D

Dagmar Rd. SL4: Wind 1C **22**
Dairy Ct. SL6: Holy 6H **13**
Daisy Mdw. TW20: Egh 4G **25**
Dalby Gdns. SL6: Maide 3G **7**
Dale Ct. SL1: Slou 1B **16**
Daleham Av. TW20: Egh 5G **25**
Dalton Grn. SL3: L'ly 5A **18**
Damson Gro. SL1: Slou 1B **16**
Dandridge Cl. SL3: L'ly 3J **17**
Danehurst Cl. TW20: Egh 5E **24**
Darkhole Ride SL4: Wink 3D **20**
Darling's La. SL6: Maide 4A **6**
Darrell Cl. SL3: L'ly 3A **18**
Dart Cl. SL3: L'ly 4C **18**
Darvill's La. SL1: Slou 1C **16**
Darwin Rd. SL3: L'ly 1A **18**
Dashwood Cl. SL3: L'ly 3H **17**
DATCHET 6G 17
DATCHET COMMON 7J 17
Datchet Pl. SL3: Dat 7G **17**
Datchet Rd. SL3: Hort 2K **23**
SL3: Slou 3E **16**
SL4: Old Win 3F **23**
SL4: Wind 6C **16**
Datchet Station (Rail) 7G 17
Daventry Cl. SL3: Poyle 7G **19**
David Lloyd Leisure
Maidenhead 6G 7
Davison Rd. SL3: L'ly 4A **18**
Dawes E. Rd. SL1: Burn 3F **9**
Dawes Moor Cl. SL2: Slou 5H **11**
Dawley Ride SL3: Poyle 7F **19**
Dawson Cl. SL4: Wind 1K **21**
Deacon Ct. SL4: Wind 1G **21**
Deal Av. SL1: Slou 5J **9**
Dean Cl. SL4: Wind 2G **21**
Deans Cl. SL2: Stoke P 7K **5**
Deansfield Cl. SL6: Maide 2E **6**
Decies Way SL2: Stoke P 7J **5**
DEDWORTH 1H 21
Dedworth Dr. SL4: Wind 7J **15**
DEDWORTH GREEN 2G 21
Dedworth Mnr. SL4: Wind 7J **15**
Dedworth Rd. SL4: Wind 1F **21**
Deena Cl. SL1: Slou 6H **9**
Deep Fld. SL3: Dat 6G **17**
Dee Rd. SL4: Wind 6F **15**
Deerswood SL6: Maide 4H **7**
Dell, The SL6: Maide 2A **12**
TW20: Eng G 2A **24**
Dell Cl. SL2: Farn C 4E **4**
Delta Way TW20: Thorpe 7J **25**
Denham Cl. SL6: Maide 6D **6**
Denham Rd. TW20: Egh 3G **25**
Denmark St. SL6: Maide 4F **7**
Dennis Way SL1: Slou 6G **9**
Denny Rd. SL3: L'ly 3A **18**
Derek Rd. SL6: Maide 4K **7**
De Ros Pl. TW20: Egh 5G **25**
Derwent Dr. SL1: Slou 4F **9**
SL6: Maide 4E **6**
Derwent Rd. TW20: Egh 6H **25**
Desborough Cres. SL6: Maide 7D **6**
Deseronto Trad. Est.
SL3: L'ly 1K **17**
Devereux Rd. SL4: Wind 1C **22**
Deverills Way SL3: L'ly 3D **18**
Devil's La. TW18: Staines 6K **25**
TW20: Egh 5J **25**
Devon Av. SL1: Slou 5B **10**
Devonshire Cl. SL2: Farn R 1A **10**
Devonshire Grn. SL2: Farn R 1A **10**
Dewar Spur SL3: L'ly 5A **18**
Dhoon Ri. SL6: Maide 6G **7**
Diamond Rd. SL1: Slou 1F **17**
Diana Cl. SL3: G Grn 5K **11**
Dickens Pl. SL3: Poyle 7F **19**
Dimsdale Dr. SL2: Farn C 4A **4**
Disraeli Ct. SL3: L'ly 5C **18**
Ditton Pk. Rd. SL3: L'ly 5K **17**
Ditton Rd. SL3: Dat 7J **17**
SL3: L'ly 4A **18**
Doddsfield Rd. SL2: Slou 2K **9**
Dolphin Ct. SL1: Slou 1G **17**
Dolphin Rd. SL1: Slou 1G **17**
Donkey La. UB7: W Dray 3K **19**
Donnington Gdns. SL6: Maide 3G **7**
Dorchester Cl. SL6: Maide 3C **6**
Dornels SL2: Slou 5H **11**
DORNEY 2E 14
Dorney Court 2E 14
Dorney Lake 4E 14
Dorney Lake Pk. & Nature Reserve
4E 14
Dorney Lake Rowing Cen. 6G 15
DORNEY REACH 2C 14
Dorney Reach Rd. SL6: Dor R 2C **14**
Dorney Wood Rd. SL1: Burn 3A **4** & 1F **9**
Dorset Rd. SL4: Wind 1B **22**
Douglas Rd. SL2: Slou 4C **10**
Dove Ho. Cres. SL2: Slou 2H **9**
Dover Rd. SL1: Slou 5J **9**
Dower Pk. SL4: Wind 3H **21**
Downing Path SL2: Slou 3H **9**
Down Pl. SL4: Wat O 5D **14**
Downs Rd. SL3: L'ly 1J **17**
Dragons Health Club
Slough 5H 9
Drake Av. SL3: L'ly 3J **17**
Drew Mdw. SL2: Farn C 3E **4**
Drift Rd. SL4: Wink 3A **20**
Drift Way SL3: Coln 7D **18**
Drive, The SL3: Dat 7G **17**
SL3: L'ly 1K **17**
TW19: Wray 4J **23**
Dropmore Rd. SL1: Burn 1F **9**
Drummond Ho. *SL4: Wind* *2C* ***22***
(off Balmoral Gdns.)
Duchess St. SL1: Slou 7H **9**
Dudley Ct. SL1: Slou 2F **17**
Duffield La. SL2: Stoke P 5H **5**
Duffield Pk. SL2: Stoke P 2F **11**
Dugdale Ho. *TW20: Egh* *4J* ***25***
(off Pooley Grn. Rd.)
Duke Pl. *SL1: Slou* *6E* ***10***
(off Montague Rd.)
Dukes Dr. SL2: Farn C 4B **4**
Dukes Kiln Dr. SL9: Ger X 1K **5**
Duke St. SL4: Wind 6B **16**
Dukes Valley SL9: Ger X 1K **5**
Dunbar Cl. SL2: Slou 6F **11**
Dunboyne Pl. SL4: Old Win 3F **23**
Duncannon Cres. SL4: Wind 2G **21**
Duncroft SL4: Wind 2J **21**
Duncroft Mnr. TW18: Staines 3K **25**
Dundee Rd. SL1: Slou 5J **9**
Dungrove Hill La.
SL6: Maide 1A **6**
Dunholme End SL6: Maide 2E **12**
Dunster Gdns. SL1: Slou 6K **9**
Dunwood Ct. SL6: Maide 7D **6**
Dupre Cl. SL1: Slou 1H **15**
Durham Av. SL1: Slou 5K **9**
Durnford Ho. *SL4: Eton* *5C* ***16***
(off Slough Rd.)
Dutch Elm Av. SL4: Wind 6E **16**
Dyson Cl. SL4: Wind 2A **22**

E

Earlsfield SL6: Holy 3K **13**
Earls La. SL1: Slou 7J **9**
Eastbourne Rd. SL1: Slou 5K **9**
Eastbridge SL2: Slou 1G **17**
EAST BURNHAM 6C 4
E. Burnham La. SL2: Farn R 7C **4**
East Cres. SL4: Wind 7J **15**
Eastcroft SL2: Slou 3A **10**
East Dr. SL2: Stoke P 2D **10**
Eastfield Cl. SL1: Slou 2F **17**
Eastfield Rd. SL1: Burn 4D **8**
East Rd. SL6: Maide 5F **7**
East Ter. SL4: Wind 7D **16**
Ebsworth Cl. SL6: Maide 1K **7**
Eden Cl. SL3: L'ly 4B **18**
Edinburgh Av. SL1: Slou 4K **9**
Edinburgh Gdns. SL4: Wind 2C **22**
Edinburgh Rd. SL6: Maide 3F **7**
Edith Rd. SL6: Maide 5B **6**
Edmunds Way SL2: Slou 4G **11**
Edwards Ct. SL1: Slou 1D **16**
Egerton Rd. SL2: Slou 3H **9**
EGHAM 4G 25
Egham Bus. Village
TW20: Thorpe 7J **25**
Egham By-Pass TW20: Egh 4F **25**
Egham Hill TW20: Egh, Eng G 5D **24**
EGHAM HYTHE 5K 25
Egham Mus. 4G 25
Egham Rdbt. TW18: Staines 4K **25**
Egham Sports Cen. 5H 25
Egham Station (Rail) 4G 25
EGHAM WICK 6A 24
Egremont Gdns. SL1: Slou 7K **9**
EGYPT 3D 4
Egypt La. SL2: Farn C 1D **4**
Eight Acres SL1: Burn 3E **8**
Elbow Mdw. SL3: Poyle 7G **19**
Elderfield Rd. SL2: Stoke P 5H **5**
Elder Way SL3: L'ly 1A **18**
Elizabeth Ct. SL1: Slou 1F **17**
SL4: Wind *1B* ***22***
(off St Leonard's Rd.)
Elizabeth Way SL2: Stoke P 7H **5**
Elkins Rd. SL2: Hedg 1G **5**
Ellesmere Cl. SL3: Dat 5F **17**
Elliman Av. SL2: Slou 6D **10**

Elliman Sq. *SL1: Slou* 1E **16**
    (off High St.)
Ellington Ct. SL6: Tap 5K **7**
Ellington Gdns. SL6: Tap 5K **7**
Ellington Pk. SL6: Maide 3F **7**
Ellington Rd. SL6: Tap 5K **7**
Ellis Av. SL1: Slou 1D **15**
Ellison Cl. SL4: Wind 2J **21**
Ellison Ho. *SL4: Wind* 7C **16**
    (off Victoria St.)
Elmar Grn. SL2: Slou 2K **9**
Elmbank Av. TW20: Eng G 5B **24**
Elm Cl. SL2: Farn C 5E **4**
Elm Cft. SL3: Dat 7H **17**
Elm Dr. SL4: Wink 7E **20**
Elm Gro. SL6: Maide 5F **7**
Elmhurst Rd. SL3: L'ly 2B **18**
Elm Rd. SL4: Wind 2A **22**
Elmshott La. SL1: Slou 6H **9**
Elmwood SL6: Maide 1J **7**
Elmwood Rd. SL2: Slou 6G **11**
Elruge Cl. UB7: W Dray 2K **19**
Eltham Av. SL1: Slou 1H **15**
Elton Dr. SL6: Maide 4E **6**
Elwell Cl. TW20: Egh 5G **25**
Ely Av. SL1: Slou 4B **10**
Embankment, The
    TW19: Wray 6H **23**
Ember Rd. SL3: L'ly 2C **18**
Emerald Ct. SL1: Slou 1D **16**
Emilia Cl. SL6: Maide 3G **7**
Emlyn Bldgs. SL4: Eton 6B **16**
Endfield Pl. SL6: Maide 6C **6**
Englefield Cl. TW20: Eng G 5C **24**
ENGLEFIELD GREEN 4C **24**
Englehurst TW20: Eng G 5C **24**
English Gdns. TW19: Wray 3J **23**
Ennerdale Cres. SL1: Slou 4F **9**
Erica Cl. SL1: Slou 6H **9**
Errington Dr. SL4: Wind 7K **15**
Eskdale Gdns. SL6: Holy 3J **13**
Essex Av. SL2: Slou 4B **10**
ETON 5C **16**
Eton Cl. SL3: Dat 5F **17**
Eton College 5C **16**
Eton Ct. SL4: Eton 6C **16**
Eton Riverside SL4: Eton 6C **16**
Eton Rd. SL3: Dat 4E **16**
Eton Sq. SL4: Eton 6C **16**
Eton Wlk. *SL1: Slou* 2D **16**
    (off Upton Pk.)
ETON WICK 3J **15**
Eton Wick Rd. SL4: Eton W 3H **15**
Evenlode SL6: Maide 4G **7**
Everard Av. SL1: Slou 1D **16**
Evergreen Oak Av.
    SL4: Wind 2F **23**
Eversley Way TW20: Thorpe 7J **25**
Eyre Grn. SL2: Slou 2K **9**

F

Fairacre SL6: Maide 6D **6**
Fairacres Ind. Est.
    SL4: Wind 1F **21**
Faircroft SL2: Slou 3A **10**
Fairfield App. TW19: Wray 5J **23**
Fairfield Av. SL3: Dat 6H **17**
Fairfield Cl. SL3: Dat 6J **17**
Fairfield La. SL2: Farn R 1A **10**
Fairfield Rd. SL1: Burn 2F **9**
    TW19: Wray 5J **23**
Fairford Rd. SL6: Maide 4G **7**
Fairhaven TW20: Egh 4F **25**
Fairhaven Ct. TW20: Egh 4F **25**
Fairlawn Pk. SL4: Wind 3H **21**
Fairlea SL6: Maide 1B **12**
Fairlie Rd. SL1: Slou 5K **9**
Fairlight Av. SL4: Wind 1C **22**
Fairview Rd. SL2: Slou 3J **9**
    SL6: Tap 5D **8**

Fairway, The SL1: Burn 1F **9**
    SL6: Maide 2C **12**
Fairway Av. UB7: W Dray 1K **19**
Falaise TW20: Egh 4E **24**
Falconwood TW20: Egh 4E **24**
Fallows, The SL6: Maide 3H **7**
Falmouth Rd. SL1: Slou 5K **9**
Fane Way SL6: Maide 1E **12**
Faraday Cl. SL2: Slou 4A **10**
Faraday Rd. SL2: Slou 4A **10**
Farm Cl. SL6: Holy 4K **13**
    SL6: Maide 5B **6**
    SL6: Tap 5D **8**
Farm Cres. SL2: Slou 4G **11**
Farm Dr. SL4: Old Win 5G **23**
Farmers Cl. SL6: Maide 1B **12**
Farmers Rd. TW18: Staines 4K **25**
Farmers Way SL6: Maide 7B **6**
Farm La. SL1: Slou 6C **10**
Farm Rd. SL6: Maide 5B **6**
    SL6: Tap 5D **8**
Farm Yd. SL4: Wind 6C **16**
Farnburn Av. SL1: Slou 4A **10**
FARNHAM COMMON 5E **4**
Farnham La. SL2: Slou 2H **9**
Farnham Pk. La. SL2: Farn R 6E **4**
Farnham Rd. SL1: Slou 2A **10**
    SL2: Farn R, Slou 2A **10**
FARNHAM ROYAL 2B **10**
Farrer Ho. *SL4: Eton* 4B **16**
    (off Common La.)
Farthingales, The SL6: Maide 5J **7**
Farthing Grn. La.
    SL2: Stoke P 1F **11**
Fawcett Rd. SL4: Wind 7A **16**
Fawley Cl. SL6: Maide 2E **6**
Fawsley Cl. SL3: Poyle 6F **19**
Feathers La. TW19: Wray 1G **25**
Ferndale Pk. SL6: Bray 5B **14**
Fern Dr. SL6: Tap 5E **8**
Fernley Ct. SL6: Maide 3E **6**
Ferrers Cl. SL1: Slou 7H **9**
Ferry End SL6: Bray 1K **13**
Ferry La. TW19: Wray 1H **25**
Ferry Rd. SL6: Bray 1K **13**
Fetty Pl. SL6: Maide 1E **12**
Fieldhurst SL3: L'ly 4A **18**
Fielding Gdns. SL3: L'ly 1H **17**
Fielding Rd. SL6: Maide 5C **6**
Fieldings, The SL6: Holy 6H **13**
Fields, The SL1: Slou 1C **16**
Field Vw. TW20: Egh 4J **25**
FIFIELD 7A **14**
Fifield La. SL4: Wink 3A **20**
Fifield Rd. SL6: Bray, Fifi 6A **14**
Fifield Way Cotts. *SL6: Fifi* 7A **14**
    (off Fifield Rd.)
Filey Spur SL1: Slou 1A **16**
Filmer Rd. SL4: Wind 1G **21**
Finch Ct. SL6: Maide 7E **6**
Firbank Pl. TW20: Eng G 5B **24**
Fircroft Cl. SL2: Stoke P 5J **5**
Fircroft Rd. TW20: Eng G 6C **24**
Firs Av. SL4: Wind 2J **21**
Firs Dr. SL3: L'ly 7K **11**
Firs La. SL6: Maide 1A **12**
First Cres. SL1: Slou 4B **10**
Fir Tree Av. SL2: Stoke P 3E **10**
FISHERY .6J **7**
Fishery Rd. SL6: Maide 7J **7**
Fishguard Spur SL1: Slou 1G **17**
Fitzrobert Pl. TW20: Egh 5G **25**
Flamborough Spur
    SL1: Slou 1K **15**
Flanders Ct. TW20: Egh 4J **25**
Fleetbrook Ho. SL3: Dat 7J **17**
Fleetwood Rd. SL2: Slou 7E **10**
Florence Av. SL6: Maide 4G **7**
Foliejohn Way SL6: Maide 3A **12**
Folkestone Ct. SL3: L'ly 4B **18**
Follett Cl. SL4: Old Win 5G **23**
Folly Way SL6: Maide 5F **7**

Fontwell Cl. SL6: Maide 4A **6**
Forbe's Ride SL4: Wink 5D **20**
Forest Grn. Rd. SL6: Fifi, Holy 7F **13**
Forest Rd. SL4: Wind 1G **21**
    (Ash La.)
    SL4: Wind 7G **21**
    (Plain Ride)
Forest Vw. Cotts. SL6: Fifi 7K **13**
Forge Dr. SL2: Farn C 5E **4**
Forlease Cl. SL6: Maide 6H **7**
Forlease Dr. SL6: Maide 6H **7**
Forlease Rd. SL6: Maide 5H **7**
Formby Cl. SL3: L'ly 3D **18**
Forsythia Gdns. SL3: L'ly 2K **17**
Foster Av. SL4: Wind 2H **21**
Fosters Path SL2: Slou 3J **9**
Fotherby Ct. SL6: Maide 6H **7**
Fotheringay Gdns. SL1: Slou 6K **9**
Foundation Pk. SL6: Maide 1A **12**
Fountain Gdns. SL4: Wind 2C **22**
Foxborough Cl. SL3: L'ly 4B **18**
Foxborough Ct. SL6: Maide 1F **13**
Foxherne SL3: L'ly 1H **17**
Foxhollow Dr. SL2: Farn C 4E **4**
Fox Rd. SL3: L'ly 3J **17**
Frances Av. SL6: Maide 3K **7**
Frances Rd. SL4: Wind 2B **22**
Francis Way SL1: Slou 6G **9**
Franklin Av. SL2: Slou 4A **10**
Franklin Cres. SL4: Wind 2G **21**
Frank Sutton Way SL1: Slou 6C **10**
Frascati Way SL6: Maide 5G **7**
Fratons, The SL6: Maide 5A **6**
Frays Av. UB7: W Dray 1K **19**
Frays Cl. UB7: W Dray 2K **19**
Freemans Cl. SL2: Stoke P 5H **5**
Freestone Yd. *SL3: Coln* 6E **18**
    (off Park St.)
Frenchum Gdns. SL1: Slou 6H **9**
Frensham Wlk. SL2: Farn C 4E **4**
Friary, The SL4: Old Win 5H **23**
FRIARY ISLAND 5H **23**
Friary Island TW19: Wray 5H **23**
Friary Rd. TW19: Wray 6H **23**
    (not continuous)
Frithe, The SL2: Slou 5G **11**
FROGMORE 2E **22**
Frogmore Border SL4: Wind 2D **22**
Frogmore Cl. SL1: Slou 1K **15**
Frogmore Dr. SL4: Wind 7D **16**
Frogmore House 1E **22**
Frymley Vw. SL4: Wind 7G **15**
Fullbrook Cl. SL6: Maide 4H **7**
Furness SL4: Wind 1F **21**
Furness Pl. SL4: Wind 1F **21**
Furness Row SL4: Wind 1F **21**
Furness Sq. SL4: Wind 1F **21**
Furness Wlk. *SL4: Wind* 1F **21**
    (off Furnace Sq.)
Furness Way SL4: Wind 1F **21**
Furnival Av. SL2: Slou 4A **10**
Furrow Way SL6: Maide 1B **12**
Furzedown Cl. TW20: Egh 5E **24**
Furzen Cl. SL2: Slou 2K **9**
FURZE PLATT 2E **6**
Furze Platt Rd. SL6: Maide 2B **6**
Furze Platt Station (Rail) 3F **7**
Furze Rd. SL6: Maide 3E **6**
Fuzzens Wlk. SL4: Wind 1H **21**

G

Gables Cl. SL3: Dat 5F **17**
    SL6: Maide 4J **7**
Gage Cl. SL6: Maide 1F **13**
Gainsborough Dr. SL6: Maide 2E **12**
Gala Bingo
    Slough 1D **16**
Galahad Cl. SL1: Slou 1K **15**
Galleons La. SL3: Wex 3H **11**
    (not continuous)

Galleymead Rd.
SL3: Poyle 7G **19**
Gallop, The SL4: Wind 6B **22**
Galloway Chase SL2: Slou 6F **11**
Gallys Rd. SL4: Wind 1G **21**
Galvin Rd. SL1: Slou 7B **10**
Garden Cl. SL6: Maide 7B **6**
Garden M. SL1: Slou 7E **10**
Garden M., The SL6: Maide 5C **6**
Gardner Ho. SL6: Maide 3F **7**
Gardner Rd. SL6: Maide 2E **6**
Garfield Pl. SL4: Wind 1C **22**
Garnet Cl. SL1: Slou 1K **15**
Garrard Rd. SL2: Slou 3H **9**
Garson La. TW19: Wray 6J **23**
Garthlands SL6: Maide 2E **6**
Gascon's Gro. SL2: Slou 3K **9**
Gas La. SL6: Bray 2H **13**
Gatehouse Cl. SL4: Wind 3A **22**
Gatewick Cl. SL1: Slou 7D **10**
Gatward Av. SL6: Maide 2C **12**
Gaveston Rd. SL2: Slou 2J **9**
Gays La. SL6: Holy 6J **13**
GEORGE GREEN 5K 11
George Grn. Dr. SL3: G Grn 5K **11**
George Grn. Rd. SL3: G Grn 5J **11**
GERRARDS CROSS NUFFIELD HOSPITAL
.... 7K 5
Gerrards Cross Rd.
SL2: Stoke P 5J **5**
Gervaise Cl. SL1: Slou 7J **9**
Gibson Ct. SL3: L'ly 4A **18**
Gilbert Way SL3: L'ly 4A **18**
Gilliat Rd. SL1: Slou 6D **10**
Gilman Cres. SL4: Wind 2G **21**
Gilmore Cl. SL3: L'ly 1H **17**
Gladstone Ind. Est.
SL6: Maide 4F ***7***
(off Denmark St.)
Gladstone Way SL1: Slou 7K **9**
Glanmor Rd. SL2: Slou 6G **11**
GLANTY 3J 25
Glanty, The TW20: Egh 3H **25**
Glebe Cl. SL6: Tap 1C **14**
Glebe Rd. SL4: Old Win 4G **23**
SL6: Maide 7J **7**
TW20: Egh 4J **25**
Glen, The SL3: L'ly 3H **17**
Glenavon Gdns. SL3: L'ly 3H **17**
Glenfields SL2: Stoke P 7H **5**
Glentworth Pl. SL1: Slou 7B **10**
Gloucester Av. SL1: Slou 4B **10**
Gloucester Dr. TW18: Staines 2J **25**
Gloucester Pl. SL4: Wind 1C **22**
Gloucester Rd. SL6: Maide 2F **7**
Godolphin Ho. *SL4: Eton 5C* ***16***
(off Common La.)
Godolphin Rd. SL1: Slou 6C **10**
Golden Ball La. SL6: Maide 1A **6**
Golden Oak Cl. SL2: Farn C 5E **4**
Goldsworthy Way SL1: Slou 5F **9**
Goodman Pk. SL2: Slou 7H **11**
Goodwin Rd. SL2: Slou 2J **9**
Goose Grn. SL2: Farn R 1A **10**
Gordon Rd. SL4: Wind 1J **21**
SL6: Maide 5E **6**
TW18: Staines 3J **25**
Gore, The SL1: Burn 2D **8**
Gore Rd. SL1: Burn 2E **8**
Goring Rd. TW18: Staines 4K **25**
Gorse Meade SL1: Slou 7A **10**
Goslar Way SL4: Wind 1A **22**
Gosling Grn. SL3: L'ly 2K **17**
Gosling Rd. SL3: L'ly 2K **17**
Goswell Hill SL4: Wind 7C **16**
Goswell Rd. SL4: Wind 7C **16**
Gowings Grn. SL1: Slou 1H **15**
Grace Ct. SL1: Slou 7B **10**
Grafton Cl. SL3: G Grn 5K **11**
SL6: Maide 2F **7**
Graham Cl. SL6: Maide 7D **6**
Grampian Way SL3: L'ly 4B **18**
Grange, The *SL1: Burn 2F* ***9***
(off Green La.)
SL4: Old Win 4G **23**
Grange Cl. TW19: Wray 5K **23**
Grange Ct. TW20: Egh 4F **25**
Grange Gdns. SL2: Farn C 4F **5**
Grange Rd. TW20: Egh 4F **25**
(not continuous)
Grangewood SL3: Wex 4H **11**
Grant Av. SL1: Slou 5D **10**
Granville Av. SL2: Slou 4C **10**
Grasholm Way SL3: L'ly 3D **18**
Grasmere SL4: Wind 6H **15**
Grasmere Av. SL2: Slou 6F **11**
Grasmere Cl. TW20: Egh 6H **25**
Grasmere Pde. SL2: Slou 6G **11**
Grassy La. SL6: Maide 5F **7**
Gratton Dr. SL4: Wind 3H **21**
Grays All. SL6: Maide 5A **6**
Grays Pk. Rd. SL2: Stoke P 1F **11**
Grays Pl. SL2: Slou 7E **10**
Gray's Rd. SL1: Slou 7E **10**
Great Hill Cres. SL6: Maide 7C **6**
Green, The SL1: Burn 4E **8**
SL1: Slou 1C **16**
SL3: Dat 6G **17**
SL6: Holy 5H **13**
TW19: Wray 5K **23**
TW20: Eng G 3C **24**
Greenacre SL4: Wind 1H **21**
Greenacre Ct. TW20: Eng G 5C **24**
Green Bus. Cen., The
TW18: Staines 3J **25**
Green Cl. SL6: Maide 3G **7**
SL6: Tap 5D **8**
Greendale M. SL2: Slou 6F **11**
Green Dr. SL3: L'ly 3K **17**
(not continuous)
SL6: Tap 1B **8**
Greenfern Av. SL1: Slou 5F **9**
Greenfield Ho. *TW20: Eng G 5B* ***24***
(off Kings La.)
Greenfields SL6: Maide 6H **7**
Green La. SL1: Burn .... 2F **9** & 6A **4**
SL2: Farn C 5D **4**
SL3: Dat 7G **17**
SL4: Wind 1K **21**
SL6: Bray, Maide 6H **7**
SL6: Fifi 7K **13**
TW18: Staines 7K **25**
TW20: Egh 3H **25**
(The Avenue)
TW20: Egh 4H **25**
(Vicarage Dr.)
TW20: Thorpe 7J **25**
Green La. Ct. SL1: Burn 2F **9**
Green Leys SL6: Maide 2G **7**
Greenock Rd. SL1: Slou 5K **9**
Green Pk. TW18: Staines 2K **25**
Greenside SL2: Slou 4K **9**
Greenway SL1: Burn 1E **8**
Greenway, The SL1: Slou 7G **9**
Greenways TW20: Egh 4E **24**
Greenways Dr. SL6: Maide 4B **6**
Gregory Dr. SL4: Old Win 5G **23**
Gregory Rd. SL2: Hedg 1F **5**
Grenfell Av. SL6: Maide 6G **7**
Grenfell Pl. SL6: Maide 6G **7**
Grenfell Rd. SL6: Maide 5F **7**
(not continuous)
Grenville Cl. SL1: Burn 1E **8**
Gresham Rd. SL1: Slou 5K **9**
Greystoke Rd. SL2: Slou 4J **9**
Griffin Cl. SL1: Slou 1B **16**
SL6: Maide 7F **7**
Gringer Hill SL6: Maide 3E **6**
Grosvenor Ct. SL1: Slou 5D **10**
Grosvenor Dr. SL6: Maide 4J **7**
Grove, The SL1: Slou 1F **17**
TW20: Egh 4G **25**
Grove Cl. SL1: Slou 2F **17**
SL4: Old Win 6G **23**
Grove Ct. TW20: Egh 4G **25**
Grove Rd. SL1: Burn 2G **9**
SL4: Wind 1B **22**
SL6: Maide 5G **7**
(not continuous)
Guards Club Rd.
SL6: Maide 5K **7**
Guards Rd. SL4: Wind 1F **21**
Guards Wlk. SL4: Wind 1F **21**
Gullet Path SL6: Maide 7E **6**
Gwendale SL6: Maide 3D **6**
Gwent Cl. SL6: Maide 1C **12**
Gwynne Cl. SL4: Wind 7H **15**
Gypsy La. SL2: Stoke P 3G **5**

H

Haddon Rd. SL6: Maide 7D **6**
Hadley Ct. *SL3: Poyle 7F* ***19***
(off Coleridge Cres.)
Hadlow Ct. SL1: Slou 7B **10**
Hag Hill La. SL6: Tap 5D **8**
Hag Hill Ri. SL6: Tap 5D **8**
Haig Dr. SL1: Slou 1A **16**
Halifax Cl. SL6: Maide 4B **6**
Halifax Rd. SL6: Maide 4B **6**
Halifax Way SL6: Maide 4B **6**
Halkingcroft SL3: L'ly 1H **17**
Hall Ct. SL3: Dat 6G **17**
Hall Mdw. SL1: Burn 1F **9**
Halse Dr. SL2: Farn C 3A **4**
Hambleden Wlk. SL6: Maide 1F **7**
Hamilton Gdns. SL1: Burn 2E **8**
Hamilton Pk. SL6: Maide 6B **6**
Hamilton Rd. SL1: Slou 5K **9**
Hamilton Way SL2: Farn C 4E **4**
HAM ISLAND 3J 23
Ham La. SL4: Old Win 4H **23**
TW20: Eng G 3B **24**
Hammond End SL2: Farn C 3D **4**
Hampden Cl. SL2: Stoke P 2F **11**
Hampden Rd. SL3: L'ly 2A **18**
SL6: Maide 4C **6**
Hampshire Av. SL1: Slou 4B **10**
Hanbury Cl. SL1: Burn 4D **8**
HAND CLINIC, THE 7F 15
Hanley Cl. SL4: Wind 7G **15**
Hanover Cl. SL1: Slou 2F **17**
SL4: Wind 7J **15**
TW20: Eng G 5B **24**
Hanover Ga. SL1: Slou 7K **9**
Hanover Mead SL6: Bray 2K **13**
Hanover Way SL4: Wind 1J **21**
Harborough Cl. SL1: Slou 7G **9**
Harcourt TW19: Wray 5K **23**
Harcourt Cl. SL6: Dor R 2C **14**
TW20: Egh 5J **25**
Harcourt Rd. SL4: Wind 7H **15**
SL6: Dor R 2C **14**
Hardell Cl. TW20: Egh 4G **25**
Harding Spur SL3: L'ly 5A **18**
Hardwick Cl. SL6: Maide 4A **6**
Hardy Cl. SL1: Slou 7K **9**
Harefield Rd. SL6: Maide 5B **6**
Harehatch La. SL1: Burn 1A **4**
SL2: Farn C 1A **4**
Hare Shoots SL6: Maide 7F **7**
Harewood Pl. SL1: Slou 2F **17**
Hargrave Rd. SL6: Maide 4E **6**
Harkness Rd. SL1: Burn 4E **8**
Harmondsworth Moor Waterside
.... 5J 19
Harmondsworth Moor Waterside Vis. Cen.
.... 5J 19
Harrington Cl. SL4: Wind 3J **21**
Harris Gdns. SL1: Slou 1B **16**
Harrison Way SL1: Slou 7G **9**
Harrogate Ct. SL3: L'ly 4B **18**
Harrow Cl. SL6: Maide 3F **7**
Harrow La. SL6: Maide 3E **6**
Harrow Mkt. SL3: L'ly 2B **18**

Harrow Rd. SL3: L'ly 2A 18
Hartland Cl. SL1: Slou 7C 10
Hartley Cl. SL3: Stoke P 7K 5
Hartley Copse SL4: Old Win 5F 23
Harvest Hill Rd.
  SL6: Bray, Maide 1F 13
Harvest Rd. TW20: Eng G 4D 24
Harvey Rd. SL3: L'ly 2C 18
Harwich Rd. SL1: Slou 5K 9
Harwood Gdns. SL4: Old Win 6G 23
Haslemere Rd. SL4: Wind 7K 15
Hasting Cl. SL6: Bray 3K 13
Hastings Mdw. SL2: Stoke P 7H 5
Hatch, The SL4: Wind 6F 15
Hatchgate Gdns. SL1: Burn 2G 9
Hatch La. SL4: Wind 2K 21
Hatfield Cl. SL6: Maide 6D 6
Hatfield Rd. SL1: Slou 1F 17
Hatton Av. SL2: Slou 3C 10
Hatton Ct. SL4: Wind 1B 22
Havelock Bus. Pk. SL6: Maide 5D 6
Havelock Cres. SL6: Maide 5C 6
Havelock Rd. SL6: Maide 5C 6
Hawker Ct. SL3: L'ly 2B 18
Hawkshill Rd. SL2: Slou 2K 9
Hawthorne Av. SL4: Wink 7E 20
Hawthorne Cres. SL1: Slou 5D 10
Hawthorne Dr. SL4: Wink 7E 20
Hawthorne Rd. TW18: Staines 4J 25
Hawthorne Way SL4: Wink 7E 20
Hawthorn Gdns. SL6: Maide 7F 7
Hawthorn Hill Rd. SL6: Pal S 7E 12
Hawthorn La. SL2: Farn C 6B 4
Hawthorns, The SL3: Poyle 7G 19
Hawtrey Cl. SL1: Slou 1G 17
Hawtrey Ho. SL4: Eton 5C 16
  (off Slough Rd.)
Hawtrey Rd. SL4: Wind 1B 22
Haymill Rd. SL1: Slou 3G 9
  SL2: Slou 3G 9
Haynes Cl. SL3: L'ly 4A 18
Hayse Hill SL4: Wind 7G 15
Haywards Mead SL4: Eton W 4J 15
Hazel Cl. TW20: Eng G 5B 24
Hazelhurst Rd. SL1: Burn 1F 9
Hazell Cl. SL6: Maide 4G 7
Hazell Way SL2: Stoke P 6H 5
Hazlemere Rd. SL2: Slou 7G 11
Headington Cl. SL6: Maide 5B 6
Headington Pl. SL2: Slou 7E 10
  (off Mill St.)
Headington Rd. SL6: Maide 4B 6
Hearne Dr. SL6: Holy 4H 13
Heathacre SL3: Coln 7F 19
Heathcote SL6: Bray 3J 13
Heathcote Ct. SL4: Wind 2C 22
  (off Osbourne Rd.)
Heatherside Gdns.
  SL2: Farn C 2F 5
Heathlands Dr. SL6: Maide 6B 6
HEATHROW AIRPORT 7K 19
Heathrow Cl. UB7: Lford 7J 19
HEDGERLEY 1F 5
HEDGERLEY HILL 1F 5
Hedgerley Hill SL2: Hedg 2F 5
Hedingham M. SL6: Maide 5E 6
Helena Rd. SL4: Wind 1C 22
Helston La. SL4: Wind 7A 16
Helvellyn Cl. TW20: Egh 6H 25
Hemming Way SL2: Slou 2A 10
Hempson Av. SL3: L'ly 2H 17
Hemsdale SL6: Maide 3C 6
Hemwood Rd. SL4: Wind 2G 21
Hencroft St. Nth. SL1: Slou 1E 16
Hencroft St. Sth. SL1: Slou 2E 16
Hendons Way SL6: Holy 4J 13
Henley Ct. TW20: Egh 3G 25
Henley Rd. SL1: Slou 5H 9
  SL6: Maide 5A 6
Henry Rd. SL1: Slou 1C 16
Heritage Ct. TW20: Egh 4G 25
  (off Station Rd.)

Hermitage Cl. SL3: L'ly 2H 17
Hermitage La. SL4: Wind 2K 21
Herndon Cl. TW20: Egh 3G 25
Heron Dr. SL3: L'ly 3C 18
Heronfield TW20: Eng G 5C 24
Herschel Pk. Dr. SL1: Slou 1E 16
Herschel Sports 6C 10
Herschel St. SL1: Slou 1E 16
Hetherington Cl. SL2: Slou 2J 9
Hever Cl. SL6: Maide 6D 6
Heynes Grn. SL6: Maide 2C 12
Heywood Av. SL6: Maide 4B 12
Heywood Cl. SL6: Maide 4B 12
Heywood Ct. Cl. SL6: Maide 3B 12
Heywood Gdns. SL6: Maide 3B 12
Hibbert Rd. SL6: Bray 2H 13
Hibbert's All. SL4: Wind 7C 16
Highfield Cl. TW20: Eng G 5C 24
Highfield Ct. SL2: Farn R 7D 4
  TW20: Eng G 5D 24
  (off Highfield Rd.)
Highfield La. SL6: Maide 1B 12
Highfield Rd. SL4: Wind 2J 21
  SL6: Maide 4C 6
  TW20: Eng G 5C 24
Highgrove Pk. SL6: Maide 4F 7
Highlands SL2: Farn C 4E 4
Highland Vw. Pk. Homes
  UB7: W Dray 3K 19
High St. SL1: Burn 2F 9
  SL1: Slou 2B 16
  (Brammas Cl.)
  SL1: Slou 1E 16
  (William St., not continuous)
  SL3: Coln 6D 18
  SL3: Dat 7G 17
  SL3: L'ly 4A 18
  SL4: Eton 5C 16
  SL4: Wind 7C 16
  SL6: Bray 1K 13
  SL6: Maide 5G 7
  (not continuous)
  SL6: Tap 3B 8
  TW19: Wray 5K 23
  TW20: Egh 4F 25
High St. W. SL1: Slou 1D 16
High Town Rd. SL6: Maide 6F 7
  (not continuous)
HIGHWAY 6C 6
Highway Av. SL6: Maide 5B 6
Highway Rd. SL6: Maide 6C 6
Hillary Rd. SL3: L'ly 1K 17
Hillersdon SL2: Slou 4G 11
Hill Farm Rd. SL6: Tap 1B 8
Hillmead Cl. SL6: Tap 4C 8
Hillrise SL3: L'ly 5B 18
Hillside SL1: Slou 1D 16
  SL6: Maide 7E 6
Hill Vw. Rd. TW19: Wray 5J 23
Hilperton Rd. SL1: Slou 1D 16
Hindhay La. SL6: Maide 1C 6
Hinksey Cl. SL3: L'ly 2C 18
Hinton Rd. SL1: Slou 6H 9
Hitcham La. SL1: Burn 2B 8
  SL6: Burn, Tap 2B 8
Hitcham Rd. SL1: Burn 4D 8
  SL6: Tap 5C 8
Hobbis Dr. SL6: Maide 6B 6
HOCKLEY HOLE 7K 5
Hockley La. SL2: Stoke P 6K 5
Hogarth Cl. SL1: Slou 6H 9
Hogfair La. SL1: Burn 2F 9
Holbrook Cl. TW20: Egh 4J 25
Holbrook Mdw.
  TW20: Egh 5J 25
Holland Ho. SL4: Eton 5B 16
  (off Common La.)
Holloway Ho. TW20: Egh 4F 25
Hollow Hill La. SL0: Iver 1D 18
Hollybush Hill
  SL2: Stoke P 6J 5

Holly Cl. SL2: Farn C 3E 4
  TW20: Eng G 5B 24
Hollycombe TW20: Eng G 3C 24
Holly Cres. SL4: Wind 1G 21
Holly Dr. SL4: Old Win 4D 22
  SL6: Maide 4G 7
Holmanleaze SL6: Maide 4H 7
Holmedale SL2: Slou 6H 11
Holmes Place Health and Fitness Club
  Slough 1F 17
Holmlea Rd. SL3: Dat 7J 17
Holmlea Wlk. SL3: Dat 7H 17
Holmwood Cl. SL6: Maide 7C 6
Holyhead M. SL1: Slou 5G 9
  (off Kelpatrick Rd.)
HOLYPORT 5J 13
Holyport Rd. SL6: Holy 5H 13
Holyport Rd. SL6: Holy 5H 13
Home Farm Way
  SL3: Stoke P 7K 5
Home Mdw. SL2: Farn R 1B 10
Homers Rd. SL4: Wind 7G 15
Homeside Cl. SL6: Maide 2F 7
Homestead Rd. SL6: Maide 1E 12
Homewood SL3: G Grn 5J 11
Hornbeam Gdns. SL1: Slou 2F 17
Horseguards Dr. SL6: Maide 5J 7
Horsemoor Cl. SL3: L'ly 3B 18
Horsham Reach SL6: Maide 2K 7
Horton Cl. SL6: Maide 3K 7
Horton Gdns. SL3: Hort 2K 23
Horton Grange SL6: Maide 3K 7
Horton Rd. SL3: Coln, Hort 7B 18
  SL3: Dat, Hort 6G 17
Household Cavalry Mus. 2A 22
Howard Av. SL2: Slou 4C 10
Howarth Rd. SL6: Maide 6H 7
Hoylake Cl. SL1: Slou 1H 15
Hubert Rd. SL3: L'ly 2J 17
Hudson Pl. SL3: L'ly 4A 18
Hughenden Cl. SL6: Maide 6D 6
Hughenden Rd. SL1: Slou 5C 10
Hull Cl. SL1: Slou 1B 16
Humber Way SL3: L'ly 3B 18
Hummer Rd. TW20: Egh 3G 25
Hungerford Av. SL2: Slou 4D 10
Hungerford Dr. SL6: Maide 1F 7
Hunstanton Cl. SL3: Coln 6D 18
Huntercombe Cl. SL6: Tap 5E 8
Huntercombe La. Nth.
  SL1: Slou 4F 9
  SL6: Tap 4F 9
Huntercombe La. Sth. SL6: Tap ...7E 8
Hunter Cl. SL1: Slou 4F 9
Hunters M. SL4: Wind 7B 16
Hunters Way SL1: Slou 7H 9
Huntingfield Way TW20: Egh 6K 25
Huntington Pl. SL3: L'ly 2C 18
Hunts La. SL6: Tap 1B 8
Hurricane Way SL3: L'ly 4C 18
Hurstfield Dr. SL6: Tap 5E 8
Hurst La. SL6: W Walt 7A 12
Hurst Rd. SL1: Slou 4G 9
Hurworth Av. SL3: L'ly 2H 17
Huxtable Gdns. SL6: Bray 4A 14
Hyde, The SL6: Maide 4G 7
Hylle Cl. SL4: Wind 7H 15
HYTHE END 1H 25
Hythe End Rd. TW19: Wray 1F 25
Hythe Fld. Av. TW20: Egh 5K 25
Hythe Pk. Rd. TW20: Egh 4J 25
Hythe Rd. TW18: Staines 4K 25

I

Ibbotson Ct. SL3: Poyle 7F 19
Ilchester Cl. SL6: Maide 7D 6
Ilex Cl. TW20: Eng G 6B 24
Illingworth SL4: Wind 2H 21
Imperial Ct. SL4: Wind 2K 21
Imperial Rd. SL4: Wind 2K 21

India Rd. SL1: Slou 1G **17**
Ingleglen SL2: Farn C 4D **4**
Ingleside SL3: Poyle 7F **19**
Inkerman Rd. SL4: Eton W 3J **15**
Institute Rd. SL6: Tap 5C **8**
In-The-Ray SL6: Maide 4J **7**
Iona Cres. SL1: Slou 5H **9**
Ipswich Rd. SL1: Slou 5J **9**
Island, The TW19: Wray 2G **25**
   UB7: Lford 6K **19**
Island Cl. TW18: Staines 3K **25**
Islet Pk. SL6: Maide 1K **7**
Islet Pk. Dr. SL6: Maide 1K **7**
Islet Pk. Ho. SL6: Maide 1A **8**
Islet Rd. SL6: Maide 1J **7**
Ismay Ct. SL2: Slou 5D **10**
Iver Station (Rail) 1G **19**
Ives Rd. SL3: L'ly 2A **18**
Ivy Cl. SL6: Holy 6H **13**
Ivy Cres. SL1: Slou 6J **9**

J

Jacob Cl. SL4: Wind 7H **15**
Jakes Ho. SL6: Maide 4H **7**
James Mdw. SL3: L'ly 5A **18**
James St. SL4: Wind 7C **16**
Jarratt Ho. SL4: Wind 2A **22**
   (off St Leonard's Rd.)
Jefferson Cl. SL3: L'ly 3B **18**
Jellicoe Cl. SL1: Slou 1A **16**
Jennery La. SL1: Burn 2F **9**
Jesus Hospital SL6: Bray 2K **13**
John F Kennedy Memorial 1C **24**
John Taylor Ct. SL1: Slou 7B **10**
Jones Way SL2: Hedg 1F **5**
Jourdelay's SL4: Eton 5C **16**
   (off Jourdelay's Pas.)
Jourdelay's Pas. SL4: Eton 5C **16**
Journeys End SL2: Stoke P 4D **10**
Jubilee Arch SL4: Wind 7C **16**
Jubilee Cotts. SL3: L'ly 4C **18**
Jubilee Way SL3: Dat 6H **17**
Judy's Pas. SL4: Eton 4B **16**
Juniper Ct. SL1: Slou 1F **17**
Juniper Dr. SL6: Maide 4J **7**
Jutland Ho. SL4: Wind 1J **21**
Jutland Pl. TW20: Egh 4J **25**

K

Kaywood Cl. SL3: L'ly 2H **17**
Keate Ho. SL4: Eton 5C **16**
   (off Keates La.)
Keates La. SL4: Eton 5B **16**
Keble Rd. SL6: Maide 4E **6**
Keel Dr. SL1: Slou 1A **16**
Keeler Cl. SL4: Wind 2H **21**
Keepers Farm Cl.
   SL4: Wind 1H **21**
   (not continuous)
Kelpatrick Rd. SL1: Slou 5G **9**
Kelsey Cl. SL6: Maide 2E **12**
Kempe Cl. SL3: L'ly 3D **18**
Kemsley Chase
   SL2: Farn R 7E **4**
Kendal Cl. SL2: Slou 6F **11**
Kendal Dr. SL2: Slou 6F **11**
Kendall Pl. SL6: Maide 1D **12**
Kendrick Rd. SL3: Slou 2G **17**
Kenilworth Cl. SL1: Slou 2E **16**
Kenneally SL4: Wind 1F **21**
Kenneally Cl. SL4: Wind 1F **21**
Kenneally Pl. SL4: Wind 1F **21**
Kenneally Row SL4: Wind 1F **21**
   (off Liddell Sq.)
Kenneally Wlk. SL4: Wind 1F **21**
   (off Guards Rd.)
Kennedy Cl. SL2: Farn C 5E **4**
   SL6: Maide 6D **6**

Kennedy Ho. SL1: Slou 7G **9**
   (off Harrison Way)
Kennet Rd. SL6: Maide 4G **7**
Kennett Rd. SL3: L'ly 2C **18**
Kent Av. SL1: Slou 4B **10**
Kentons La. SL4: Wind 1H **21**
Kent Way SL6: Maide 3F **7**
Kenwood Cl. SL6: Maide 5B **6**
Keppel Spur SL4: Old Win 6G **23**
Kepple St. SL4: Wind 1C **22**
Kestrel Path SL2: Slou 3H **9**
Keswick Ct. SL2: Slou 6E **10**
Keswick Rd. TW20: Egh 6H **25**
Kidderminster Rd. SL2: Slou 2K **9**
Kidwells Cl. SL6: Maide 5G **7**
Kidwells Pk. Dr. SL6: Maide 5G **7**
Killarney Dr. SL6: Maide 5F **7**
Kiln Cl. SL2: Hedg 1E **4**
Kiln Pl. SL6: Maide 1B **6**
Kimber Cl. SL4: Wind 2K **21**
Kimberley Cl. SL3: L'ly 3A **18**
Kimbers Dr. SL1: Burn 2G **9**
Kimbers La. SL6: Maide 2F **13**
Kinburn Dr. TW20: Egh 4E **24**
King Acre Ct. TW18: Staines ...2K **25**
King Edward VII Av. SL4: Wind .6D **16**
King Edward Ct. SL4: Wind 7C **16**
King Edward Ct. Shop. Cen.
   SL4: Wind 7B **16**
KING EDWARD VII HOSPITAL 2B **22**
King Edward St. SL1: Slou 1C **16**
Kingfisher Ct. SL2: Slou 3A **10**
Kinghorn La. SL6: Maide 1E **6**
Kinghorn Pk. SL6: Maide 1E **6**
King John La. TW19: Wray 4J **23**
King John's Cl. TW19: Wray 4J **23**
Kingsbury Cres. TW18: Staines ..3K **25**
Kingsbury Dr. SL4: Old Win 6F **23**
Kingsfield SL4: Wind 7G **15**
Kings Gro. SL6: Maide 6F **7**
Kings Gro. Ind. Est.
   SL6: Maide 6F **7**
Kings La. TW20: Eng G 4A **24**
Kingsley Av. TW20: Eng G 5B **24**
Kingsley Path SL2: Slou 3G **9**
Kingsmead Ho. SL1: Slou 7B **10**
Kingsoak Ct. SL6: Maide 2C **12**
Kings Rd. SL1: Slou 2D **16**
   SL4: Wind 3C **22**
   TW20: Egh 3G **25**
King Stable St. SL4: Eton 6C **16**
Kings Ter. SL3: L'ly 5C **18**
King St. SL6: Maide 5G **7**
   (not continuous)
Kingsway SL2: Farn C 5D **4**
Kingsway M. SL2: Farn C 5D **4**
Kingswood Cl. TW20: Eng G 3D **24**
Kingswood Ct. SL6: Bray 7G **7**
Kingswood Creek
   TW19: Wray 4J **23**
Kingswood Ho. SL2: Slou 4B **10**
Kingswood Ri. TW20: Eng G 4D **24**
Kinnaird Ct. SL1: Tap 5F **9**
Kipling Ct. SL4: Wind 1A **22**
Kirkwall Spur SL1: Slou 4D **10**
Knightsbridge Ct. SL3: L'ly 3B **18**
   (off High St.)
Knights Cl. SL4: Wind 7G **15**
   TW20: Egh 5K **25**
Knights Pl. SL4: Wind 2B **22**
Knolton Way SL2: Slou 5G **11**
Knowsley Cl. SL6: Maide 3B **6**
Kola Ct. SL2: Slou 5G **11**
Kotan Dr. TW18: Staines 3J **25**

L

Laburnham Rd. SL6: Maide 6E **6**
Laburnum Gro. SL3: L'ly 5C **18**
Laburnum Pl. TW20: Eng G 5B **24**
Lacey Cl. TW20: Egh 6K **25**

Ladbrooke Rd. SL1: Slou 2B **16**
Lady Astor Ct. SL1: Slou 1D **16**
Ladyday Pl. SL1: Slou 7B **10**
LA Fitness
   Slough 1E **16**
Laggan Rd. SL6: Maide 2G **7**
Laggan Sq. SL6: Maide 3G **7**
Lake Av. SL1: Slou 6C **10**
LAKE END 1E **14**
Lake End Ct. SL6: Maide 5D **8**
Lake End Rd. SL4: Dor 2E **14**
   SL6: Dor R, Tap 6E **8**
Lakeside SL6: Maide 2J **7**
Lakeside Dr. SL2: Stoke P 7G **5**
Lakeside Ind. Est. SL3: Coln 5G **19**
Lakeside SL0: Rich P 6G **19**
   SL3: Coln, Rich P 6G **19**
Lake Vw. SL6: Maide 3H **7**
Lakeview Pk. Cvn. Site
   SL4: Wink 7B **20**
Lambert Av. SL3: L'ly 2K **17**
Lambourne Dr. SL6: Maide 2D **12**
Lambton Ho. SL4: Wind 2K **21**
Lammas Av. SL4: Wind 1B **22**
Lammas Cl. TW18: Staines 2K **25**
Lammas Ct. SL4: Wind 1B **22**
   TW19: Staines 1K **25**
Lammas Dr. TW18: Staines 3K **25**
Lammas Rd. SL1: Slou 4G **9**
Lancaster Av. SL2: Slou 3B **10**
Lancaster Cl. TW20: Eng G 4D **24**
Lancaster Rd. SL6: Maide 4C **6**
Lancastria M. SL6: Maide 5E **6**
Lancelot Cl. SL1: Slou 1K **15**
Langdale Cl. SL6: Maide 6H **7**
Langdown Way SL6: Maide 7E **6**
Langham Pl. TW20: Egh 4F **25**
LANGLEY 2B **18**
Langley Broom SL3: L'ly 4A **18**
Langley Bus. Cen. SL3: L'ly 1B **18**
Langley Bus. Pk. SL3: L'ly 1B **18**
Langley Leisure Cen. 3C **18**
Langley Pk. Country Pk. 4K **11**
Langley Pk. Rd. SL3: L'ly 1B **18**
Langley Quay SL3: L'ly 1B **18**
Langley Rd. SL1: Slou 1H **17**
LANGLEY RDBT. 4B **18**
Langley Station (Rail) 1B **18**
Langton Cl. SL1: Slou 7G **9**
   SL6: Maide 3E **6**
Langton's Mdw. SL2: Farn C 5E **4**
Langton Way TW20: Egh 5J **25**
Langworthy End SL6: Holy 5J **13**
Langworthy La. SL6: Holy 5H **13**
Lansdowne Av. SL1: Slou 7D **10**
Lansdowne Ct. SL1: Slou 7D **10**
Lantern Wlk. SL6: Maide 5J **7**
   (off The Farthingales)
Larch Cl. SL2: Slou 4A **10**
Larchfield Rd. SL6: Maide 7E **6**
Larchmoor Pk. SL2: Stoke P 4J **5**
Larchwood Dr. TW20: Eng G 5B **24**
Larkings La. SL2: Stoke P 7K **5**
Larksfield TW20: Eng G 6B **24**
La Roche Cl. SL3: L'ly 2H **17**
Lascelles Rd. SL3: Slou 2G **17**
Lassell Ct. SL6: Maide 4J **7**
Lassell Gdns. SL6: Maide 5J **7**
Laurel Av. SL3: L'ly 1K **17**
   TW20: Eng G 4B **24**
Laurel Cl. SL3: Poyle 6F **19**
Lawkland SL2: Farn R 2B **10**
Lawn Av. UB7: W Dray 1K **19**
Lawn Cl. SL3: Dat 6H **17**
Lawns, The SL3: Poyle 7F **19**
Lawrence Cl. SL4: Wind 1B **22**
Lawrence Way SL1: Slou 4F **9**
Laxton Grn. SL6: Maide 2D **12**
Layburn Cres. SL3: L'ly 5C **18**
Lea, The TW20: Egh 6J **25**
Leaholme Gdns. SL1: Slou 4F **9**
Ledger La. SL6: Fifi 1A **20**

Ledgers Rd. SL1: Slou 1C 16
Leeds Rd. SL1: Slou 6D 10
Lee La. SL6: Maide 1A 6
Lees Cl. SL6: Maide 7C 6
Lees Gdns. SL6: Maide 7C 6
Leeson Gdns. SL4: Eton W 3H 15
Legoland .4G 21
Leigh Pk. SL3: Dat 6G 17
Leigh Rd. SL1: Slou 6A 10
Leigh Sq. SL4: Wind 1G 21
Leighton Gdns. SL6: Maide 3J 7
Leiston Spur SL1: Slou 5D 10
Leith Cl. SL1: Slou 7F 11
LENT 3E 8
Lent Grn. SL1: Burn 3E 8
(not continuous)
Lent Grn. La. SL1: Burn 3E 8
LENT RISE .4E 8
Lent Ri. Rd. SL1: Burn 5E 8
SL6: Tap 5E 8
Lerwick Dr. SL1: Slou 4D 10
Leslie Dunne Ho. SL4: Wind 1H 21
Lewes Ct. SL1: Slou 2B 16
Lewins Farm Ct. SL1: Slou 6J 9
Lewins Way SL1: Slou 6J 9
Leworth Pl. SL4: Wind 7C 16
Lexington Av. SL6: Maide 7E 6
Liddell SL4: Wind 2F 21
Liddell Pl. SL4: Wind 1F 21
Liddell Sq. SL4: Wind 1F 21
Liddell Way SL4: Wind 2F 21
Lidstone Ct. SL3: G Grn 5J 11
Lilac Ct. SL2: Slou 2J 9
Lilley Way SL1: Slou 7H 9
Lillibrooke Cres.
SL6: Maide 2B 12
Lily Dr. UB7: W Dray 3K 19
Lime Av. SL4: Wind 7E 16
Limes, The SL4: Wind 1F 21
Limes M. TW20: Egh 4F 25
Limes TW20: Egh 4F 25
Lime Wlk. SL6: Maide 4B 6
Linchfield Rd. SL3: Dat 7H 17
Lincoln Ct. SL1: Slou 2D 16
Lincoln Hatch La. SL1: Burn 3F 9
Lincoln Rd. SL6: Maide 4C 6
Lincoln Way SL1: Slou 6G 9
Linden SL3: L'ly 4C 18
Linden Av. SL6: Maide 3E 6
Linden Ct. TW20: Eng G 5B 24
Linden Dr. SL2: Farn R 7E 4
Lindores Rd. SL6: Holy 5J 13
Lingholm Cl. SL6: Maide 6D 6
Link, The SL2: Slou 5G 11
Link Rd. SL3: Dat 7H 17
Linkswood Rd. SL1: Burn 1F 9
Lismore Pk. SL2: Slou 5E 10
Litcham Spur SL1: Slou 5C 10
Littlebrook Av. SL2: Slou 3H 9
Little Buntings SL4: Wind 2J 21
Lit. Chapels Way SL1: Slou 1K 15
Littlecroft Rd. TW20: Egh 4F 25
Littledown Rd. SL1: Slou 7E 10
LITTLEFIELD GREEN 7A 12
Littlefield Grn. SL6: W Walt 7A 12
Littleport Spur SL1: Slou 5D 10
Lit. Sutton La. SL3: L'ly 5C 18
(Kings Ter.)
SL3: L'ly 4D 18
(Sutton La.)
Little Woodlands SL4: Wind 2J 21
LITTLEWORTH COMMON 2A 4
Littleworth Rd. SL1: Burn 1A 4
Liverpool Rd. SL1: Slou 5A 10
Lochinvar Cl. SL1: Slou 1A 16
Lock Av. SL6: Maide 2K 7
Lockbridge Ct. SL6: Maide 4J 7
Locke Gdns. SL3: L'ly 1H 17
Lockets Cl. SL4: Wind 7G 15
Lock La. SL6: Maide 1D 12
Lock Mead SL6: Maide 2K 7
Lock Path SL4: Dor, Eton W 5G 15

Loddon Dr. SL6: Maide 4E 6
Loddon Spur SL1: Slou 6D 10
Lodge Cl. SL1: Slou 1B 16
TW20: Eng G 4D 24
Lodge Way SL4: Wind 2H 21
LONDON-HEATHROW AIRPORT 7K 19
London Rd. GU25: Vir W 7B 24
SL3: Dat 6G 17
(not continuous)
SL3: L'ly 2H 17
TW20: Eng G 7B 24
Longbourn SL4: Wind 2K 21
Long Cl. SL2: Farn C 6D 4
Long Dr. SL1: Burn 2F 9
Longfield SL2: Hedg 2F 5
LONGFORD 7J 19
Longford Cir. UB7: Lford 7J 19
LONGFORDMOOR 7H 19
Long Furlong Dr. SL2: Slou 3G 9
Long La. SL6: Holy, Pal S 7F 13
Longleat Gdns. SL6: Maide 6E 6
Longmead SL4: Wind 7H 15
Long Readings La. SL2: Slou 2A 10
Longside Cl. TW20: Egh 7J 25
Long Wlk., The SL4: Wind 7C 22
Longwood Av. SL3: L'ly 4C 18
Longworth Dr. SL6: Maide 3K 7
Lonsdale Cl. SL6: Maide 3H 7
Lonsdale Way SL6: Holy 4K 13
Look Ahead SL1: Slou 1D 16
Loosen Dr. SL6: Maide 2B 12
Lord Mayor's Dr. SL2: Farn C 5B 4
(not continuous)
Lord Raglan Ho. SL4: Wind 2B 22
Loring Rd. SL4: Wind 7J 15
Lorne Cl. SL1: Slou 2A 16
Lorne Ct. SL1: Slou 2B 16
Losfield Rd. SL4: Wind 7H 15
Lotus Pk. TW18: Staines 3K 25
Lovegrove Dr. SL2: Slou 3J 9
Lovejoy La. SL4: Wind 1G 21
Lovett Gdns. SL6: Maide 1J 7
Lovett Rd. TW18: Staines 3H 25
Lowbrook Dr. SL6: Maide 2B 12
Lwr. Boyndon Rd. SL6: Maide 6F 7
Lwr. Britwell Rd. SL2: Slou 3G 9
(not continuous)
Lwr. Cippenham La. SL1: Slou 7H 9
Lwr. Cookham Rd. SL6: Maide 1K 7
Lwr. Lees Rd. SL2: Slou 2K 9
Lowestoft Dr. SL1: Slou 5G 9
Luddington Av. GU25: Vir W 7F 25
Ludlow Rd. SL6: Maide 6F 7
Luff Cl. SL4: Wind 2H 21
Lundy Ct. SL1: Slou 6H 9
Lutman La. SL6: Maide 2G 7
Lydford Av. SL2: Slou 4C 10
Lydsey Cl. SL2: Slou 2K 9
Lyell Pl. E. SL4: Wind 2F 21
Lyell Pl. W. SL4: Wind 2F 21
Lyell Rd. SL4: Wind 2F 21
Lyell Wlk. E. SL4: Wind 2F 21
Lyell Wlk. W. SL4: Wind 2F 21
LYNCH HILL 2H 9
Lynch Hill La. SL2: Slou 3H 9
Lynden Cl. SL6: Holy 5J 13
Lyndwood Dr. SL4: Old Win 5F 23
Lyndwood Pde. SL4: Old Win 5F 23
(off St Luke's Rd.)
Lyneham Gdns. SL6: Maide 3C 6
Lyngfield Cvn. Pk. SL6: Bray 5A 14
Lynton Grn. SL6: Maide 5F 7
Lynwood Av. SL3: L'ly 2J 17
TW20: Egh 5E 24
Lysander Mead SL6: Maide 4K 7

M

McAuliffe Dr. SL2: Farn C 3B 4
Mackenzie Mall SL1: Slou 1E 16
(off Wellington St.)

Mackenzie St. SL1: Slou 1E 16
Madeira Wlk. SL4: Wind 7C 16
Mafeking Rd. TW19: Wray 1H 25
Magna Carta La. TW19: Wray 7J 23
Magna Carta Monument 1D 24
Magna Rd. TW20: Eng G 5B 24
Magnet Leisure Cen. 5H 7
Magnolia Gdns. SL3: L'ly 2H 17
Magpie Way SL2: Slou 3J 9
MAIDENHEAD 5G 7
Maidenhead Bri. SL6: Maide 5K 7
Maidenhead Bus. Campus, The
SL6: Maide 2A 12
MAIDENHEAD COURT 1K 7
Maidenhead Ct. Pk. SL6: Maide 1J 7
MAIDENHEAD HUNTERCOMBE HOSPITAL
. . . . .6F 9
Maidenhead Retail Pk.
SL6: Maide 6H 7
Maidenhead Rd. SL4: Wind 6F 15
SL6: Maide 2F 7
Maidenhead Sailing Club 2H 7
Maidenhead Station (Rail) 6G 7
Maidenhead United FC 6G 7
Main Dr. SL0: Rich P 3F 19
Main Rd. SL4: Wind 6F 15
Majors Farm Rd. SL3: Dat 6J 17
Malders La. SL6: Maide 1B 6
Malet Cl. TW20: Egh 5K 25
Mallard Cl. SL1: Burn 1E 8
Mallard Dr. SL1: Slou 6J 9
Mallow Pk. SL6: Maide 3D 6
Malpas Rd. SL2: Slou 6G 11
Malt Hill TW20: Egh 4E 24
Malt Ho. Cl. SL4: Old Win 6G 23
Maltings, The TW18: Staines 3K 25
Malton Av. SL1: Slou 5A 10
Malvern Ct. SL3: L'ly 5B 18
Malvern Rd. SL6: Maide 3E 6
Mandeville Ct. TW20: Egh 3G 25
Manfield Ct. SL2: Slou 2K 9
Manor Ct. SL1: Slou 7J 9
TW18: Staines 4K 25
Manorcrofts Rd. TW20: Egh 5G 25
Mnr. Farm Cl. SL4: Wind 2J 21
Mnr. Farm Cotts. SL4: Old Win 4F 23
Mnr. Farm Ct. TW20: Egh 4G 25
MANOR FARM ESTATE 6H 23
Mnr. Farm Ho. SL4: Wind 2J 21
Mnr. Farm La. TW20: Egh 4G 25
Manor Gro. SL6: Fifi 7A 14
Manor Ho. SL4: Eton 5C 16
(off Common La.)
Manor Ho. La. SL3: Dat 6G 17
Manor La. SL6: Maide 1F 13
Manor Leaze TW20: Egh 4H 25
MANOR PARK 4C 10
Manor Pk. TW18: Staines 2K 25
Manor Rd. SL4: Wind 1H 21
SL6: Maide 1F 13
Manor Way SL6: Holy 5H 13
TW20: Egh 5F 25
Mansel Cl. SL2: Slou 4G 11
Mansell Cl. SL4: Wind 7H 15
Mansion Cvn. Site SL0: Iver 1D 18
Mansion La. SL0: Iver 1D 18
Maple Cl. SL6: Maide 7D 6
Maple Ct. SL4: Wind 2B 22
TW20: Eng G 5B 24
Maple Cres. SL2: Slou 6G 11
Mapledurham Wlk. SL6: Maide 1F 7
Maplin Pk. SL3: L'ly 1C 18
Marbeck Cl. SL4: Wind 7G 15
Marcia Ct. SL1: Slou 7J 9
Marescroft Rd. SL2: Slou 3H 9
Marina Way SL1: Slou 6G 9
Marish Cl. SL3: L'ly 2B 18
Marish Wharf SL3: L'ly 1K 17
Market La. SL3: L'ly 2D 18
Market Pl. SL3: Coln 6D 18
Market St. SL4: Wind 7C 16
SL6: Maide 5G 7

Marlborough Cl. SL6: Maide 6B 6
Marlborough Rd. SL3: L'ly 3J 17
  SL6: Maide 6B 6
Marlow Rd. SL6: Maide 5G 7
  (Bad Godesberg Way)
  SL6: Maide 1A 6
  (Lee La.)
Marshall Hall TW20: Eng G 2C 24
  (off Coopers Hill La.)
Marshfield SL3: Dat 7H 17
Marshgate Trad. Est. SL6: Tap 5D 8
Marsh La. SL4: Dor 1C 14
  SL6: Dor, Dor R, Tap 7B 8
Martin Cl. SL4: Wind 7F 15
Martin Rd. SL1: Slou 2D 16
  SL6: Maide 4G 7
Martin's Plain SL2: Stoke P 2E 10
Marunden Grn. SL2: Slou 2J 9
Mary Drew Almshouses
  TW20: Eng G 5D 24
Mary Morgan Ct. SL2: Slou 4C 10
Maryside SL3: L'ly 1K 17
Mascoll Path SL2: Slou 2J 9
Masons Ct. SL1: Slou 6H 9
Masons Rd. SL1: Slou 6H 9
Mathisen Way SL3: Poyle 7F 19
Maudsley Ho. SL6: Maide 5H 7
Mausoleum 2E 22
Maybury Cl. SL1: Slou 5G 9
Mayfield Cvn. Pk.
  UB7: W Dray 2K 19
Mayfield Dr. SL4: Wind 2K 21
Mayflower Way SL2: Farn C 4E 4
Maynard Cl. SL4: Wind 7K 15
Maypole Rd. SL6: Tap 4D 8
Mead Av. SL3: L'ly 1C 18
Mead Cl. SL3: L'ly 1C 18
  TW20: Egh 5H 25
Mead Ct. TW20: Egh 5J 25
Meadfield Av. SL3: L'ly 1B 18
Meadfield Rd. SL3: L'ly 2B 18
Meadowbank SL6: Maide 7B 6
Meadowbrook SL3: Poyle 7G 19
Meadow Cl. SL4: Old Win 4G 23
Meadow Ct. TW18: Staines 2K 25
Meadow Gdns. TW18: Staines 4K 25
Meadow La. SL4: Eton W 5A 16
Meadow Rd. SL3: L'ly 2K 17
Meadow Vw. La. SL6: Holy 5F 13
Meadow Way SL4: Old Win 5G 23
  SL6: Dor R 1C 14
  SL6: Fifi .7A 14
Meads, The SL4: Wind 1K 21
Mead Wlk. SL3: L'ly 1C 18
Mead Way SL1: Slou 4G 9
Medallion Pl. SL6: Maide 5J 7
Mede Cl. TW19: Wray 7J 23
Mede Ct. TW18: Staines 2K 25
Medlake Pl. TW20: Egh 6J 25
Medlake Rd. TW20: Egh 5J 25
Medlar Ct. SL2: Slou 7H 11
Megabowl
  Maidenhead 4G 7
Melbourne Av. SL1: Slou 5B 10
Mellor Wlk. SL4: Wind 7C 16
  (off Batchelors Acre)
Melton Ct. SL6: Maide 6G 7
  (off Cullerns Pas.)
Mendip Cl. SL3: L'ly 4B 18
Mercian Way SL1: Slou 7G 9
Mercia Rd. SL6: Maide 1C 12
Mere Rd. SL1: Slou 2E 16
Merlin Cl. SL3: L'ly 5C 18
Merlin Ct. SL6: Maide 4C 6
Merton Cl. SL6: Maide 2D 12
Merton Rd. SL1: Slou 2F 17
Merwin Way SL4: Wind 1G 21
Meryton Ho. SL4: Wind 2K 21
Mews, The TW20: Eng G 3D 24
  (off Coopers Hill La.)
Michael Cl. SL6: Maide 7D 6
Midcroft SL2: Slou 3A 10

MIDDLE GREEN 7K 11
Middle Grn. SL3: L'ly 7K 11
Middlegreen Rd. SL3: L'ly 1J 17
Middlegreen Trad. Est.
  SL3: L'ly 1J 17
Middle Hill TW20: Egh, Eng G 3C 24
Middle Wlk. SL1: Burn 2E 8
Mildenhall Rd. SL1: Slou 5D 10
Milford Ct. SL1: Slou 1F 17
Millbrook Way SL3: Poyle 7F 19
Mill Cl. UB7: W Dray 2K 19
Mill Ct. SL2: Slou 7E 10
Millers Ct. TW20: Egh 5K 25
Miller's La. SL4: Old Win 5E 22
Mill La. SL4: Wind 6K 15
  SL6: Tap 5K 7
Mill Pl. SL3: Dat 1J 23
Mill Pl. Cvn. Pk. SL3: Dat 1H 23
Mill Rd. UB7: W Dray 2K 19
Millside Ct. SL0: Thorn 1J 19
Millside Pk. SL4: Wink 7C 20
Mills Spur SL4: Old Win 6G 23
Millstream La. SL1: Slou 7H 9
Mill St. SL2: Slou 7E 10
  SL3: Coln 6E 18
Mill West SL2: Slou 7E 10
Milner Rd. SL1: Burn 4D 8
Milton Rd. SL2: Slou 3C 10
  TW20: Egh 4F 25
Milverton Cl. SL6: Maide 2C 12
Mina Av. SL3: L'ly 1J 17
Minniecroft Rd. SL1: Burn 2E 8
Minster Way SL3: L'ly 1A 18
Minton Ri. SL6: Tap 5E 8
Mirador Cres. SL2: Slou 6G 11
Misbourne Ct. SL3: L'ly 3B 18
Missenden Gdns. SL1: Burn 5E 8
Mitchell Cl. SL1: Slou 2K 15
Moat Dr. SL2: Slou 4H 11
Moffy Hill SL6: Maide 2F 7
Molyns M. SL1: Slou 7H 9
Money La. UB7: W Dray 2K 19
MONEYROW GREEN 6H 13
Moneyrow Grn. SL6: Holy 7G 13
Monkey Island La. SL6: Bray 5B 14
Monkey Island La. SL6: Bray 2A 14
Monksfield Way SL2: Slou 3K 9
Monks Rd. SL4: Wind 1G 21
Mons Wlk. TW20: Egh 4J 25
Montague Rd. SL1: Slou 6E 10
Montagu Rd. SL3: Dat 7G 17
Montem La. SL1: Slou 7C 10
Montem Leisure Cen. 1C 16
Montgomery Pl. SL2: Slou 5H 11
Montpelier Ct. SL4: Wind 1B 22
Montrose Av. SL1: Slou 5A 10
  (not continuous)
  SL3: Dat 6H 17
Montrose Dr. SL6: Maide 6B 6
Montrose Way SL3: Dat 7J 17
Monycrower Dr. SL6: Maide 5F 7
MOOR, THE 1K 25
Moorbridge Rd. SL6: Maide 5H 7
Moore Cl. SL1: Slou 1A 16
Moore Gro. Cres. TW20: Egh 5K 25
Moor End SL6: Holy 4K 13
Moores La. SL4: Eton W 3J 15
Moorfield Ter. SL6: Maide 4H 7
Moor Furlong SL1: Slou 7G 9
Moorings, The SL4: Wind 6F 15
MOOR JUNC. 6J 19
Moorland Rd. UB7: Harm 5K 19
Moorlands Dr. SL6: Maide 4A 6
Moor La. SL6: Maide 3G 7
  TW18: Staines 2K 25
  TW19: Staines 1K 25
  UB7: Harm 5K 19
Moorside Cl. SL6: Maide 3G 7
Moorstown Ct. SL1: Slou 1D 16
Moray Dr. SL2: Slou 5F 11
Moreau Wlk. SL3: G Grn 5K 11
Moreland Av. SL3: Coln 6D 18

Moreland Cl. SL3: Coln 6D 18
Morello Dr. SL3: L'ly 1A 18
Moreton Way SL1: Slou 7G 9
Morley Cl. SL3: L'ly 1A 18
Morrice Cl. SL3: L'ly 3A 18
Morris Ct. SL4: Wind 7H 15
Mortimer Rd. SL3: L'ly 2J 17
Morton Dr. SL2: Farn C 4A 4
Mossy Va. SL6: Maide 3E 6
Moundsfield Way SL1: Slou 1H 15
Mountbatten Cl. SL1: Slou 2F 17
Mountbatten Sq. SL4: Wind 7B 16
Mount Cl. SL2: Farn C 3E 4
Mount Hill La. SL9: Ger X 1K 5
Mount Lee TW20: Egh 4F 25
Mounts Hill SL4: Wink 7F 21
Mowbray Cres. TW20: Egh 4G 25
Muddy La. SL2: Slou 4D 10
Mulberry Av. SL4: Wind 2E 22
Mulberry Dr. SL3: L'ly 4K 17
Mulberry Wlk. SL6: Maide 4D 6
Mullens Rd. TW20: Egh 4H 25
Mundesley Spur SL1: Slou 5D 10
Mundy Ct. SL4: Eton 5C 16
Murrin Rd. SL6: Maide 4D 6
Mus. of Eton Life 5C 16
Mustians SL4: Eton 5B 16
  (off Eton Wick Rd.)
Myers Dr. SL2: Farn C 4D 4
MYRKE 3E 16
Myrke, The SL3: Dat 3E 16
Myrtle Cl. SL3: Poyle 7F 19
Myrtle Cres. SL2: Slou 6E 10

N

Napier Rd. SL6: Maide 6C 6
Nash Rd. SL3: L'ly 3A 18
Natural History Mus.
  Eton 5C 16
Needham Cl. SL4: Wind 7H 15
Nelson Cl. SL3: L'ly 3J 17
Nelson Rd. SL4: Wind 2J 21
Neptune Way SL1: Slou 1H 15
Neve Ho. SL6: Maide 4G 7
Neville Cl. SL2: Stoke P 5H 5
Neville Ct. SL1: Burn 2F 9
Newbeach Ho. SL2: Slou 2A 10
Newberry Cres. SL4: Wind 1G 21
Newbery Way SL1: Slou 1C 16
Newbury Dr. SL6: Maide 6J 7
Newchurch Rd. SL2: Slou 4J 9
New Cut SL1: Burn 3D 8
Newhaven Spur SL2: Slou 3A 10
Newlands Dr. SL6: Maide 5B 6
Newnham Cl. SL2: Slou 7E 10
Newport Rd. SL2: Slou 3H 9
New Rd. SL3: Dat 7J 17
  SL3: L'ly 2B 18
  SL6: Holy 5J 13
  TW18: Staines 4J 25
New Sq. SL1: Slou 1D 16
New Sta. Ho. SL1: Slou 7E 10
Newton Cl. SL3: L'ly 1A 18
Newton Ct. SL4: Old Win 5F 23
Newton La. SL4: Old Win 5G 23
Newtonside Orchard
  SL4: Old Win 5F 23
New Wickham La. TW20: Egh 6G 25
NEW WINDSOR 2C 22
NHS WALK-IN CENTRE (SLOUGH) . . .2E 16
  (in Upton Hospital)
Nicholas Gdns. SL1: Slou 7H 9
Nicholls SL4: Wind 2F 21
Nicholls Wlk. SL4: Wind 2F 21
Nicholson M. TW20: Egh 4G 25
  (off Nicholson Wlk.)
Nicholsons Cen.
  SL6: Maide 5G 7
  (off Nicholsons Wlk.)
Nicholsons La. SL6: Maide 5G 7

Nicholsons Wlk. SL6: Maide 5G 7
Nicholson Wlk. TW20: Egh 4G 25
Nightingale Ct. SL1: Slou 2F 17
Nightingale La. SL6: Maide 1E 6
Nightingale Pk. SL2: Farn G 6B 4
Nightingale Shott TW20: Egh 5F 25
Nightingale Wlk. SL4: Wind 2B 22
Nine Acres SL1: Slou 7J 9
Nixey Cl. SL1: Slou 1F 17
Noble Ct. SL2: Slou 7E 10
(off Mill St.)
Nobles Way TW20: Egh 5E 24
Norden Cl. SL6: Maide 1D 12
Norden Farm Cen. for the Arts 7D 6
Norden Mdws. SL6: Maide 7D 6
Norden Rd. SL6: Maide 7D 6
Norelands Dr. SL1: Burn 1F 9
Norfolk Av. SL1: Slou 4B 10
Norfolk Pk. Cotts. SL6: Maide 4G 7
Norfolk Rd. SL6: Maide 4F 7
Normandy Wlk. TW20: Egh 4J 25
Normans, The SL2: Slou 5G 11
Norreys Dr. SL6: Maide 1D 12
Northampton Av. SL1: Slou 5B 10
Northborough Rd. SL2: Slou 3K 9
Nth. Burnham Cl. SL1: Burn 1E 8
North Cl. SL4: Wind 7J 15
Northcroft SL2: Slou 3A 10
Northcroft Cl. TW20: Eng G 4B 24
Northcroft Gdns. TW20: Eng G 4B 24
Northcroft Rd. TW20: Eng G 4B 24
Northcroft Vs. TW20: Eng G 4B 24
North Dean SL6: Maide 3G 7
North Dr. SL2: Stoke P 2D 10
Northern Rd. SL2: Slou 3C 10
Northfield Rd. SL4: Eton W 3J 15
SL6: Maide 3G 7
North Grn. SL1: Slou 6D 10
SL6: Maide 3G 7
Northmead Rd. SL2: Slou 3J 9
North Pk. SL0: Rich P 2D 18
North Rd. SL6: Maide 5F 7
Nth. Star La. SL6: Maide 6D 6
North St. SL4: Wink 7E 20
TW20: Egh 4F 25
North Ter. SL4: Wind 6C 16
NORTH TOWN 3G 7
Nth. Town Cl. SL6: Maide 3G 7
Nth. Town Mead SL6: Maide 3G 7
Nth. Town Moor SL6: Maide 2G 7
Nth. Town Rd. SL6: Maide 3G 7
Northumbria Rd. SL6: Maide 1C 12
Norway Dr. SL2: Slou 4G 11
Notley End TW20: Eng G 6C 24
Nursery La. SL3: L'ly 7J 11
Nursery Pl. SL4: Old Win 5G 23
Nursery Rd. SL6: Tap 5E 8
Nursery Way TW19: Wray 5J 23

O

Oak Av. TW20: Egh 6J 25
Oaken Gro. SL6: Maide 4C 6
Oakfield Av. SL1: Slou 7A 10
Oakhurst SL6: Maide 1J 7
Oak La. SL4: Wind 7K 15
TW20: Eng G 2C 24
Oakley Cres. SL1: Slou 6D 10
OAKLEY GREEN 1E 20
Oakley Grn. Rd.
SL4: Oak G, Wat O 1B 20
(not continuous)
Oakridge Pl. SL2: Farn C 3E 4
Oak Stubbs La. SL6: Dor R 1C 14
Oak Tree Dr. TW20: Eng G 4C 24
Oaktree Dr. SL3: L'ly 4C 18
Oakwood Ct. SL1: Slou 5D 10
(off Mildenhall Rd.)
Oast Ho. Cl. TW19: Wray 6K 23
Oatlands Dr. SL1: Slou 5C 10
Oban Ct. SL1: Slou 1C 16

Observatory Shop. Cen., The
SL1: Slou 1F 17
Ockwells Rd. SL6: Maide 2C 12
Odencroft Rd. SL2: Slou 2K 9
Odeon Cinema
Maidenhead 6G 7
Oldacres SL6: Maide 5J 7
Old Beaconsfield Rd.
SL2: Farn C 5E 4
Old Court Cl. SL6: Maide 2C 12
Old Courtyard, The TW20: Egh 5F 25
Old Crown SL1: Slou 1E 16
Oldershaw M. SL4: Wind 4C 6
Old Ferry Dr. TW19: Wray 5H 23
Oldfield Rd. SL6: Maide 6J 7
Old Fives Ct. SL1: Burn 2E 8
Old Forge Cl. SL6: Bray 2H 13
Old House Ct. SL3: Wex 4J 11
Old Kiln Ind. Est. SL6: Maide 1B 6
Old Marsh La. SL6: Tap 1C 14
Old Mill La. SL6: Bray 1K 13
Old Nursery Ct. SL2: Hedg 1E 4
Old School Ct. TW19: Wray 6K 23
Old School M. TW18: Staines 4K 25
Old Slade La. SL0: Rich P 2F 19
SL3: Coln 4G 19
Oldway La. SL1: Slou 6G 9
(not continuous)
OLD WINDSOR 5F 23
Old Windsor Lock SL4: Old Win 4H 23
Olivia Dr. SL3: L'ly 4A 18
Omega Way TW20: Thorpe 7J 25
One Pin La. SL2: Farn C 3E 4
Opal Ct. SL3: Wex 3H 11
Opeck's Cl. SL2: Stoke P 3G 11
SL2: Wex 3G 11
Opendale Rd. SL1: Burn 4E 8
Orchard Av. SL1: Slou 4G 9
SL4: Wind 7K 15
Orchard Bungs. SL2: Farn C 6B 4
Orchard Cl. SL6: Bray 2H 13
TW20: Egh 4H 25
Orchard Ct. UB7: Lford 6K 19
Orchard Ga. SL2: Farn C 4E 4
Orchard Gro. SL6: Maide 5D 6
Orchard Lodge SL1: Slou 7H 9
(off Streamside)
Orchard Rd. SL4: Old Win 5G 23
Orchards Res. Pk. SL3: L'ly 7K 11
Orchardville SL1: Burn 3E 8
Orchard Way SL3: L'ly 7K 11
Orchid Ct. TW20: Egh 3H 25
Orwell Cl. SL4: Wind 2C 22
Osborne Cl. SL4: Wind 1B 22
Osborne M. SL4: Wind 1B 22
Osborne Rd. SL4: Wind 1B 22
TW20: Egh 5F 25
Osborne St. SL1: Slou 1E 16
Osier Pl. TW20: Egh 5J 25
Osney Rd. SL6: Maide 2F 7
Ostler Ga. SL6: Maide 3D 6
Ouseley Lodge SL4: Old Win 6H 23
(off Ouseley Rd.)
Ouseley Rd. SL4: Old Win 6H 23
(not continuous)
TW19: Wray 6H 23
Owen Cl. SL3: L'ly 4A 18
Oxford Av. SL1: Burn 1E 8
SL1: Slou 4J 9
Oxford Rd. SL4: Wind 7B 16
Oxford Rd. E. SL4: Wind 7B 16

P

Padbury Oaks UB7: Lford 7J 19
Paddock, The SL3: Dat 7G 17
SL4: Wink 6B 20
(Crouch La.)
SL4: Wink 7E 20
(Squirrel La.)
SL6: Maide 2D 6

Paddock Cl. SL6: Maide 3B 12
Padstow Cl. SL3: L'ly 1K 17
Paget Dr. SL6: Maide 1B 12
Paget Rd. SL3: L'ly 3A 18
Pagoda, The SL6: Maide 3J 7
Palace Cl. SL1: Slou 7J 9
PALEY STREET 7C 12
Paley St. SL6: Pal S 7C 12
Palmers Cl. SL6: Maide 2B 12
Palmerston Av. SL3: Slou 2G 17
Pamela Row SL6: Holy 5H 13
Pantile Row SL3: L'ly 3B 18
Parade, The SL4: Wind 7G 15
TW18: Staines 4K 25
(off Thorpe Rd.)
Parish La. SL2: Farn C 1D 4
Park & Ride
Windsor (Home Park) 5D 16
Windsor (Legoland) 4H 21
Park Av. TW19: Wray 4J 23
TW20: Egh 5J 25
Park Cl. SL4: Wind 1C 22
Park Cnr. SL4: Wind 2H 21
Parkgate SL1: Burn 3F 9
Parkland Av. SL3: L'ly 3J 17
Park La. SL1: Burn 1A 4
SL3: Coln 2G 17
SL4: Wink 7E 20
Park Lawn SL2: Farn R 2B 10
Park Ride SL4: Wind 6G 21
Park Rd. SL2: Farn R, Stoke P 1B 10
TW20: Egh 3G 25
Parkside SL6: Maide 3E 6
Parkside Lodge SL3: Slou 2F 17
(off Upton Ct. Rd.)
Parkside Wlk. SL1: Slou 2F 17
Park Sq. SL4: Wink 7E 20
Park St. SL1: Slou 2E 16
(not continuous)
SL3: Coln 7E 18
SL4: Wind 7C 16
SL6: Maide 5G 7
Parkview Chase SL1: Slou 5H 9
Parlaunt Rd. SL3: L'ly 3B 18
(not continuous)
Parry Grn. Nth. SL3: L'ly 3A 18
Parry Grn. Sth. SL3: L'ly 3B 18
Parsonage La.
SL2: Farn C, Farn R 5E 4
SL4: Wind 7K 15
Parsonage Rd. TW20: Eng G 4D 24
Parsons Rd. SL3: L'ly 4A 18
Parson's Wood La. SL2: Farn C 6F 5
Partridge Mead SL6: Maide 2G 7
Patricia Cl. SL1: Slou 6H 9
Paul Ct. TW20: Egh 4K 25
Paxton Av. SL1: Slou 2B 16
Pearce Cl. SL6: Maide 3G 7
Pearce Rd. SL6: Maide 3G 7
Pearl Gdns. SL1: Slou 7A 10
Peartree Cl. SL1: Slou 7J 9
Peascod Pl. SL4: Wind 7C 16
(off Peascod St.)
Peascod St. SL4: Wind 7B 16
Peel Cl. SL4: Wind 2A 22
Peel Ct. SL1: Slou 4A 10
Pegasus Ct. TW20: Egh 4H 25
Pelham Ct. SL6: Maide 5F 7
Pelling Hill SL4: Old Win 6G 23
Pemberley Lodge SL4: Wind 2K 21
Pemberton Rd. SL2: Slou 3H 9
Pendeen Ct. SL1: Slou 7K 9
Penn Ho. SL1: Burn 2F 9
SL4: Eton 4C 16
(off Common La.)
Pennine Rd. SL2: Slou 4K 9
Penn Mdw. SL2: Stoke P 7H 5
Penn Rd. SL2: Slou 3C 10
SL3: Dat 7J 17
Pennylets Grn. SL2: Stoke P 6H 5
Penrose Ct. TW20: Eng G 5D 24
(not continuous)

Penshurst Rd. SL6: Maide 7E 6
Pentland Rd. SL2: Slou 4K 9
Penwood Ct. SL6: Maide 5C 6
Penyston Rd. SL6: Maide 5D 6
Penzance Spur SL2: Slou 3A 10
Pepler Way SL1: Burn 2E 8
Pepys Cl. SL3: L'ly 5C 18
Percy Pl. SL3: Dat 7G 17
Perrycroft SL4: Wind 2H 21
Perryfields Way SL1: Burn 3E 8
Perry Ho. SL1: Burn 3E 8
Perryman Way SL2: Slou 2J 9
Perth Av. SL1: Slou 5A 10
Perth Trad. Est. SL1: Slou 4A 10
Peterhead M. SL3: L'ly 4B 18
Petersfield Av. SL2: Slou 7F 11
Peters La. SL6: Holy 5J 13
Petty Cross SL1: Slou 5H 9
Petworth Ct. SL4: Wind 7K 15
Pevensey Rd. SL2: Slou 4K 9
Pheasants Cft. SL6: Maide 1B 12
Philbe M. SL1: Slou 1J 15
Phipps Cl. SL6: Maide 3B 12
Phipps Rd. SL1: Slou 4G 9
(not continuous)
Phoenix Ct. SL6: Maide 1E 12
Pickford Dr. SL3: L'ly 7K 11
Pickfords Gdns. SL1: Slou 7D 10
Pierson Rd. SL4: Wind 7G 15
Pine Cl. SL6: Maide 5C 6
Pinehurst TW20: Eng G 6C 24
Piner Cotts. SL4: Wind 2H 21
Pines, The SL3: L'ly 1A 18
Pine Trees Bus. Pk.
  TW18: Staines 4K 25
Pine Way TW20: Eng G 5B 24
Pink La. SL1: Burn 1E 8
Pinkneys Dr. SL6: Maide 5A 6
PINKNEYS GREEN 3A 6
Pinkneys Rd. SL6: Maide 3B 6
Pipers Cl. SL1: Burn 2F 9
Pitts Rd. SL1: Slou 7B 10
Plackett Way SL1: Slou 7G 9
Plaines Cl. SL1: Slou 7J 9
Plain Ride SL4: Wind 7F 21
Plough La. SL2: Stoke P 7K 5
Ploughlees La. SL1: Slou 6D 10
Pluto Cl. SL1: Slou 1H 15
Plymouth Rd. SL1: Slou 4H 9
Pococks La. SL4: Eton 4D 16
Points, The SL6: Maide 2C 12
Pollard Cl. SL4: Old Win 4G 23
Pond Rd. TW20: Egh 5J 25
Pooley Av. TW20: Egh 4H 25
POOLEY GREEN 4J 25
Pooley Grn. Cl. TW20: Egh 4J 25
Pooley Grn. Rd. TW20: Egh 4H 25
Pool La. SL1: Slou 6D 10
Poolmans Rd. SL4: Wind 2G 21
Popes Cl. SL3: Coln 6C 18
Poplar Cl. SL3: Poyle 7F 19
Poplar Ho. SL3: L'ly 4A 18
Poplars Gro. SL6: Maide 2J 7
Portland Bus. Cen. SL3: Dat 7G 17
(off Manor Ho. La.)
Portland Cl. SL2: Slou 3G 9
Portlock Rd. SL6: Maide 5D 6
Portsmouth Ct. SL1: Slou 6D 10
Post Office La. SL3: G Grn 5J 11
Poulcott TW19: Wray 5K 23
Pound, The SL1: Burn 3G 9
Powerleague Soccer Cen.
  Slough 2C 16
Powis Cl. SL6: Maide 1C 12
Powney Rd. SL6: Maide 5D 6
POYLE 7F 19
Poyle La. SL1: Burn 1E 8
Poyle New Cotts. SL3: Poyle 7G 19
Poyle Rd. SL3: Poyle 7F 19
Poynings, The SL0: Rich P 3G 19
Precinct, The TW20: Egh 4G 25
Precincts, The SL1: Burn 3E 8

Preston Rd. SL2: Slou 6H 11
Prestwood SL2: Slou 5G 11
Priest Hill SL4: Old Win 2C 24
  TW20: Eng G, Old Win 2C 24
Primrose Dr. UB7: W Dray 3K 19
Primrose La. SL6: Holy 7H 13
Prince Albert's Wlk. SL4: Wind 7F 17
Prince Andrew Cl. SL6: Maide 4J 7
Prince Andrew Rd. SL6: Maide 3J 7
Prince Consort Cotts. SL4: Wind 1C 22
Prince Consort's Dr. SL4: Wind 5J 21
Princes Cl. SL4: Eton W 4J 15
Princes Rd. TW20: Slou 5F 25
Princess Av. SL4: Wind 2A 22
PRINCESS MARGARET BMI HOSPITAL
  . . . . .1C 22
Princess St. SL6: Maide 6G 7
Princes St. SL1: Slou 1G 17
Priors Cl. SL1: Slou 2F 17
  SL6: Bray 3J 13
Priors Rd. SL4: Wind 2G 21
Priors Way SL6: Bray 3J 13
Priors Way Ind. Est. SL6: Bray 3J 13
Priory Ct. TW20: Egh 5J 25
Priory Rd. SL1: Slou 4F 9
Priory Way SL3: Dat 6G 17
Progress Bus. Cen. SL1: Slou 5G 9
Prospect La. TW20: Eng G 4A 24
Prospect Pl. SL4: Wind 2C 22
(off Osbourne Rd.)
Providence Pl. SL6: Maide 5G 7
Prune Hill TW20: Egh, Eng G 6D 24
Pumpkin Hill SL1: Burn 5A 4
Pursers Ct. SL2: Slou 5D 10
Pursell Cl. SL6: Maide 2B 12
Purton Ct. SL2: Farn R 6E 4
Purton La. SL2: Farn C, Farn R 6E 4

Q

Quantock Cl. SL3: L'ly 4B 18
Quaves Rd. SL3: Slou 2G 17
Queen Adelaide's Ride SL4: Wink 5G 21
Queen Anne's Rd. SL4: Wind 3B 22
(not continuous)
Queen Ann's Ct. SL4: Wind 7C 16
(off Peascod St.)
Queen Charlotte St. SL4: Wind 7C 16
(off High St.)
Queen Elizabeth's Wlk.
  SL4: Wind 1D 22
Queens Acre SL4: Wind 3C 22
Queens Acre Ho. SL4: Wind 2C 22
Queen's Cl. SL4: Old Win 4F 23
Queens Cl. SL1: Slou 6E 10
Queen's Dr. SL3: Ful, Wex 1K 11
Queens Ga. Cotts. SL4: Wind 3C 22
Queensmead SL3: Dat 6G 17
Queensmere Rd. SL1: Slou 1E 16
Queensmere Shop. Cen.
  SL1: Slou 1E 16
  SL3: Dat 6G 17
  SL4: Eton W 4J 15
  SL4: Wind 1B 22
  TW20: Egh 4F 25
Queens Ter. SL4: Wind 2C 22
Queen St. SL6: Maide 6G 7
(not continuous)
Queensway SL6: Maide 3F 7
Queen Victoria Wlk. SL4: Wind 7D 16
Quelmans Head Ride SL4: Wind 7G 21
Quinbrookes SL2: Slou 5H 11
Quincy Rd. TW20: Egh 4G 25

R

Radcot Av. SL3: L'ly 2C 18
Radcot Cl. SL6: Maide 1F 7
Radnor Way SL3: L'ly 3K 17

Ragstone Rd. SL1: Slou 2D 16
Railway Ter. SL2: Slou 7E 10
  TW18: Staines 4K 25
Rainsborough Chase
  SL6: Maide 2C 12
Raleigh Cl. SL1: Slou 7K 9
Ralston Ct. SL4: Wind 7C 16
(off Russell St.)
Rambler Cl. SL6: Tap 5E 8
Rambler La. SL3: L'ly 2H 17
Ramsey Ct. SL2: Slou 3G 9
Randall Cl. SL3: L'ly 4A 18
Randall Ct. SL4: Old Win 5F 23
(off Lyndwood Dr.)
Randolph Rd. SL3: L'ly 2K 17
Ranelagh SL4: Wink 7E 20
Ravenfield TW20: Eng G 5C 24
Ravens Fld. SL3: L'ly 1J 17
Ravensworth Rd. SL2: Slou 2K 9
Ray Dr. SL6: Maide 5J 7
Ray Lea Cl. SL6: Maide 4J 7
Ray Lea Rd. SL6: Maide 3J 7
Ray Lodge M. SL6: Maide 5J 7
Ray Mead Cl. SL6: Maide 3K 7
Ray Mdw. SL6: Maide 3H 7
Ray Mead Rd. SL6: Maide 5K 7
Ray Mill Rd. E. SL6: Maide 3H 7
Ray Mill Rd. W. SL6: Maide 4G 7
Raymond Cl. SL3: Poyle 7F 19
Raymond Rd. SL3: L'ly 2B 18
  SL6: 5E 6
Rayners Cl. SL3: Coln 6D 18
Ray Pk. Av. SL6: Maide 3J 7
Ray Pk. La. SL6: Maide 5J 7
Ray Pk. Rd. SL6: Maide 4J 7
Ray's Av. SL4: Wind 6J 15
Ray St. SL6: Maide 5J 7
Rectory Cl. SL2: Farn R 2B 10
  SL4: Wind 7K 15
Rectory Rd. SL6: Tap 3A 8
Red Cottage M. SL3: L'ly 2H 17
Red Ct. SL1: Slou 7D 10
Reddington Dr. SL3: L'ly 3K 17
Redford Rd. SL4: Wind 7G 15
Redriff Cl. SL6: Maide 6E 6
Redwood SL1: Burn 1E 8
Redwood Gdns. SL1: Slou 6C 10
Redwoods, The SL4: Wind 2C 22
Reed Hall TW20: Eng G 2C 24
(off Coopers Hill La.)
Reedham Rd. SL1: Burn 2F 9
Reeve Rd. SL6: Holy 5J 13
Refectory Hall
  TW20: Eng G 2C 24
(off Coopers Hill La.)
Reform Rd. SL6: Maide 5J 7
Regal Ct. SL6: Bray 3J 13
Regent Ct. SL1: Slou 5D 10
  SL4: Wind 7C 16
  SL6: Maide 5G 7
Regents Pl. SL6: Maide 5D 6
Reid Av. SL6: Maide 7F 7
Repton Cl. SL6: Maide 2D 12
Retreat, The SL6: Fifi 6A 14
  TW20: Eng G 4D 24
Revesby Cl. SL6: Maide 2E 12
Rhodes Cl. TW20: Egh 4H 25
Rhodes Ct. TW20: Egh 4J 25
(off Pooley Grn. Cl.)
Ribstone Rd. SL6: Maide 2C 12
Ricardo Rd. SL4: Old Win 5G 23
Richards Way SL1: Slou 7H 9
RICHINGS PARK 1G 19
Richings Pl. SL0: Rich P 2F 19
Richings Way SL0: Rich P 2F 19
Richmond Cres. SL1: Slou 7F 11
Rickman's La. SL2: Stoke P 5G 5
Ridgebank SL1: Slou 6J 9
Ridge Ct. SL4: Wind 2B 22
Ridgemead Rd. TW20: Eng G 2A 24
Riding Ct. Farm SL3: Dat 5G 17
Riding Ct. Rd. SL3: Dat, L'ly 6H 17

Ridings, The SL0: Rich P .3G 19
SL4: Wind .6F 15
SL6: Maide .5B 6
Rigby Lodge SL1: Slou .5D 10
Ripley Av. TW20: Egh .5E 24
Ripley Cl. SL3: L'ly .3K 17
RIPLEY SPRINGS .5E 24
Risborough Rd. SL6: Maide .4F 7
Riseley Rd. SL6: Maide .5E 6
Riverbank, The SL4: Wind .6A 16
River Ct. SL6: Tap .5K 7
River Gdns. SL6: Bray .1A 14
River Pk. Av. TW18: Staines .3K 25
River Rd. SL4: Wind .6F 15
SL6: Tap .6K 7
Riverside TW19: Wray .6H 23
TW20: Egh .2G 25
Riverside Pk. SL3: Poyle .7F 19
Riverside Wlk. *SL4: Wind .6C 16*
(off Thames Side)
River St. SL4: Wind .6C 16
Rixman Cl. SL6: Maide .7E 6
Rixon Cl. SL3: G Grn .5K 11
Roasthill La. SL4: Dor .5G 15
Robert Rd. SL2: Hedg .1F 5
Roberts Way TW20: Eng G .6C 24
Robin Hood Cl. SL1: Slou .7J 9
Robin Pde. SL2: Farn C .4E 4
Robin Willis Way SL4: Old Win .5F 23
Rochester Rd. TW18: Staines .5K 25
Rochfords Gdns. SL2: Slou .6H 11
Rochford Way SL6: Tap .6D 8
Rockall Ct. SL3: L'ly .2C 18
Rodney Way SL3: Poyle .7F 19
Roebuck Grn. SL1: Slou .7H 9
Rogers La. SL2: Stoke P .6H 5
Rokesby Rd. SL2: Slou .2J 9
Rolls La. SL6: Holy .5F 13
Romney Lock SL4: Wind .5D 16
Romney Lock Rd. SL4: Wind .6C 16
Romney Wlk. SL4: Wind .6C 16
Romsey Cl. SL3: L'ly .2A 18
Romsey Dr. SL2: Farn C .2F 5
Ronaldsay Spur SL1: Slou .4D 10
Rosehill Ct. SL1: Slou .2F 17
Roseleigh Cl. SL6: Maide .5B 6
Roses La. SL4: Wind .1G 21
Rose Wlk. SL2: Slou .4A 10
Rosewood Way SL2: Farn C .4E 4
Rosken Gro. SL2: Farn R .1A 10
Rossiter Cl. SL3: L'ly .3K 17
Ross Rd. SL6: Maide .7E 6
Roundway TW20: Egh .4J 25
Rowan Av. TW20: Egh .4J 25
Rowan Hall *TW20: Eng G .2C 24*
(off Coopers Hill La.)
Rowanhurst Dr. SL2: Farn C .4E 4
Rowan Way SL2: Slou .4A 10
Rowland Cl. SL4: Wind .2G 21
Rowley La. SL3: Wex .1J 11
Roxborough Way SL6: Maide .2A 12
Roxwell Cl. SL1: Slou .7H 9
Royal Free Ct. *SL4: Wind .7C 16*
(off Bachelors Acre)
Royal Holloway
(University of London) .5D 24
Royal Holloway University Sports Cen.
.6E 24
Royal Mausoleum .2D 22
Royal M. SL4: Wind .7C 16
Royal Windsor Racecourse .5H 15
Roydon Ct. TW20: Egh .5K 25
Royston Way SL1: Slou .4G 9
Ruby Cl. SL1: Slou .1K 15
Ruddlesway SL4: Wind .1G 21
(not continuous)
Rudsworth Cl. SL3: Coln .7E 18
Runnemede Rd. TW20: Egh .3F 25
RUNNYMEDE .1D 24
Runnymede .1D 24
Runnymede Ct. TW20: Egh .3G 25
Runnymede Rdbt. TW20: Egh .3H 25
Ruscombe Gdns. SL3: Dat .6F 17
Rusham Ct. TW20: Egh .5G 25
Rusham Pk. Av. TW20: Egh .5F 25
Rusham Rd. TW20: Egh .5F 25
Rushes, The SL6: Maide .6J 7
Rushington Av. SL6: Maide .6G 7
Rushmere Pl. TW20: Eng G .4E 24
Russell Ct. SL6: Maide .5G 7
Russell St. SL4: Wind .7C 16
Russet Rd. SL6: Maide .2D 12
Rutherford Cl. SL4: Wind .7J 15
Rutland Av. SL1: Slou .4B 10
Rutland Ga. SL6: Maide .6D 6
Rutland Pl. SL6: Maide .6D 6
Rutland Rd. SL6: Maide .6E 6
Rycroft SL4: Wind .2J 21
Rydal Way TW20: Egh .6H 25
Rydings SL4: Wind .2J 21
Rye Cl. SL6: Maide .1B 12
Rye Ct. SL1: Slou .2F 17
Rylstone Cl. SL6: Maide .2D 12
Ryvers End SL3: L'ly .2A 18
Ryvers Rd. SL3: L'ly .2A 18

S

Sadlers M. SL6: Maide .5J 7
Saffron Cl. SL3: Dat .7G 17
St Adrians Cl. SL6: Maide .1C 12
St Alban's Cl. SL4: Wind .7C 16
St Alban's St. SL4: Wind .7C 16
St Andrew's Av. SL4: Wind .1J 21
St Andrew's Cl. SL4: Old Win .5F 23
TW19: Wray .5K 23
St Andrews Cotts. *SL4: Wind .1K 21*
(off Cross Oak)
St Andrews Ct. *SL1: Slou .2D 16*
(off Upton Pk.)
St Andrew's Cres. SL4: Wind .1J 21
St Andrew's Way SL1: Slou .6G 9
St Bernards Rd. SL3: L'ly .2H 17
St Catherines Pl. TW20: Egh .4G 25
St Chads Rd. SL6: Maide .1C 12
St Cloud Way SL6: Maide .5G 7
St Columbas Cl. SL6: Maide .1C 12
St Cuthberts Cl. TW20: Eng G .5D 24
St Davids Cl. SL6: Maide .1B 12
St Davids Dr. TW20: Eng G .6C 24
St Elmo Cl. SL2: Slou .3C 10
St Elmo Cres. SL2: Slou .3C 10
St Georges Chapel .7C 16
St Georges Cl. SL4: Wind .7H 15
St George's Cres. SL1: Slou .6G 9
St Ives Rd. SL6: Maide .5H 7
St James Pl. SL1: Slou .5F 9
St James Wlk. SL0: Rich P .1F 19
St John's Ct. TW20: Egh .4G 25
St John's Dr. SL4: Wind .1K 21
St Johns Rd. SL2: Slou .6F 11
SL4: Wind .1K 21
St Jude's Cl. TW20: Eng G .4C 24
St Jude's Cotts. TW20: Eng G .4C 24
St Judes Rd. TW20: Eng G .2C 24
St Laurence Way SL1: Slou .2F 17
St Leonard's Av. SL4: Wind .1B 22
St Leonard's Hill SL4: Wind .3G 21
St Leonard's Rd. SL4: Wind .2K 21
SL4: Wink .5F 21
St Leonards Wlk. SL0: Rich P .2G 19
St Luke's Rd. SL4: Old Win .5F 23
SL6: Maide .5G 7
St Margarets Rd. SL6: Maide .5B 6
St Mark's Cres. SL6: Maide .5C 6
ST MARK'S HOSPITAL .5D 6
St Marks Pl. SL4: Wind .1B 22
St Marks Rd. SL4: Wind .1B 22
SL6: Maide .5D 6
St Martin's Rd. UB7: W Dray .2K 19
St Mary's Cl. SL6: Maide .5H 7
St Mary's Rd. SL3: L'ly .7K 11
St Mary's Wlk. SL6: Maide .5G 7
St Michaels Ct. SL2: Slou .3G 9
St Nazaire Cl. TW20: Egh .4J 25
St Patricks Cl. SL6: Maide .1C 12
St Pauls Av. SL2: Slou .6E 10
St Paul's Rd. TW18: Staines .4K 25
St Peter's Cl. SL1: Burn .3E 8
SL4: Old Win .4F 23
St Peters Rd. SL4: Old Win .4F 23
SL6: Maide .2E 6
St Thomas Wlk. SL3: Coln .6E 18
Salisbury Av. SL2: Slou .3B 10
Salters Cl. SL6: Maide .5H 7
Salters Rd. SL6: Maide .5J 7
SALT HILL .7B 10
Salt Hill Av. SL1: Slou .7B 10
Salt Hill Dr. SL1: Slou .7B 10
Salt Hill Mans. SL1: Slou .7B 10
Salt Hill Way SL1: Slou .7B 10
Sampson's Grn. SL2: Slou .2J 9
Sandisplatt Rd. SL6: Maide .6B 6
Sandlers End SL2: Slou .3A 10
Sandown Rd. SL2: Slou .4J 9
Sandringham Ct. SL1: Slou .5G 9
Sandringham Rd. SL6: Maide .2F 7
Sands Farm Dr. SL1: Burn .3F 9
Sandy Mead SL6: Holy .4K 13
Sarsby Dr. TW19: Wray .1G 25
Satis Ho. SL3: Dat .6H 17
Savill M. TW20: Eng G .5D 24
Savoy Ct. SL6: Maide .3G 7
Sawyers Cl. SL4: Wind .6H 15
SL6: Maide .3B 12
Sawyers Cres. SL6: Maide .3B 12
Saxon Cl. SL3: L'ly .1A 18
Saxon Gdns. SL6: Tap .3A 8
Saxon Way SL4: Old Win .5G 23
UB7: Harm .5K 19
Saxon Way Ind. Est. UB7: Harm .5K 19
Scafell Rd. SL2: Slou .3J 9
Scarborough Way SL1: Slou .2A 16
Scholars Wlk. SL3: L'ly .1B 18
School Allotment Ride
SL4: Wink .6E 20
School La. SL2: Slou .6E 10
SL2: Stoke P .6K 5
SL6: Maide .3F 7
TW20: Egh .4G 25
School Rd. UB7: Harm .5K 19
School Wlk. SL2: Slou .6G 11
Schroder Ct. TW20: Eng G .4B 24
Scotlands Dr. SL2: Farn C .5D 4
Scott Cl. SL2: Farn C .4E 4
Seacourt Rd. SL3: L'ly .3C 18
Second Cres. SL1: Slou .4B 10
Sefton Cl. SL2: Stoke P .7H 5
Sefton Paddock SL2: Stoke P .6J 5
Sefton Pk. SL2: Stoke P .6J 5
Selim Ct. *SL1: Slou .1G 17*
(off Clifton Rd.)
Selwyn Cl. SL4: Wind .1G 21
Selwyn Pl. SL1: Slou .6J 9
Sermed Ct. SL2: Slou .7H 11
Servite Ho. SL6: Maide .4K 7
Severn Cres. SL3: L'ly .4C 18
Seymour Cl. SL6: Maide .2C 12
Seymour Ho. SL3: L'ly .1K 17
Seymour Rd. SL1: Slou .1B 16
Shackleton Rd. SL1: Slou .6E 10
Shaftesbury Ct. SL1: Slou .1D 16
Shaggy Calf La. SL2: Slou .6F 11
Sharman Row SL3: L'ly .4A 18
Sharney Av. SL3: L'ly .2C 18
Shaw Ct. SL4: Old Win .4F 23
SHAW FARM .3D 22
Shaw Gdns. SL3: L'ly .4A 18
Sheehy Way SL2: Slou .6G 11
Sheepcote Rd. SL4: Eton W .4K 15
SL4: Wind .1H 21
Sheephouse Rd. SL6: Maide .3J 7
Sheet St. SL4: Wind .1C 22
Sheet St. Rd. SL4: Wind .7J 21
Sheffield Rd. SL1: Slou .5B 10

Shelley Cl. SL3: L'ly .4A **18**
Shelton Ct. SL3: L'ly .2H **17**
Shenston Ct. *SL4: Wind .7C 16*
(off James St.)
Shenstone Dr. SL1: Burn .3G **9**
Shepherds Ct. SL4: Wind .1H **21**
Sherborne Cl. SL3: Poyle .7F **19**
Sherbourne Dr. SL4: Wind .3J **21**
SL6: Maide .2D **12**
Sherbourne Wlk. SL2: Farn C .3E **4**
Sheridan Ct. SL1: Slou .6H **9**
Sherman Rd. SL1: Slou .4D **10**
Sherwood Cl. SL3: L'ly .2K **17**
Sherwood Ct. SL3: L'ly .4A **18**
Sherwood Dr. SL6: Maide .6B **6**
Shifford Cres. SL6: Maide .2F **7**
Shirley Av. SL4: Wind .7J **15**
Shirley Rd. SL6: Maide .7D **6**
Shoppenhangers Rd. SL6: Maide .2C **12**
Shop Rd. SL4: Wind .6F **15**
Shoreham Ri. SL2: Slou .3G **9**
Shortfern SL2: Slou .5H **11**
Sidney Rd. SL4: Wind .2F **21**
Siebel Ct. TW20: Egh .3H **25**
Silco Dr. SL6: Maide .6F **7**
Silver Cl. SL6: Maide .7B **6**
Silverstone M. SL6: Maide .1D **12**
Silvertrees Dr. SL6: Maide .7B **6**
Simmons Cl. SL3: L'ly .3B **18**
Simons Wlk. TW20: Eng G .6C **24**
Simpson Cl. SL6: Maide .4J **7**
Simpsons Way SL1: Slou .7C **10**
Sinclair Rd. SL4: Wind .2B **22**
Sir Henry Peakes Dr. SL2: Farn C .5C **4**
Sir Robert M. SL3: L'ly .4B **18**
Sir Sydney Camm Ho.
SL4: Wind .7A **16**
Skerries Ct. SL3: L'ly .3B **18**
Sky Bus. Cen. TW20: Thorpe .7J **25**
Skydmore Path SL2: Slou .2J **9**
Skye Lodge *SL1: Slou .7D 10*
(off Lansdowne Av.)
Skyport Dr. UB7: Harm .6K **19**
SLOUGH .1F **17**
Slough Crematorium SL2: Slou .4E **10**
Slough Ice Arena .7C **10**
Slough Ind. Est. SL1: Slou .4K **9**
(not continuous)
Slough Interchange Ind. Est.
SL2: Slou .7F **11**
Slough Mus. .1F **17**
Slough Retail Pk. SL1: Slou .7A **10**
Slough Rd. SL1: Slou .3D **16**
SL3: Dat .4F **17**
SL4: Eton .5C **16**
Slough Station (Rail) .7E **10**
Slough Supapitch .4G **11**
Slough Tennis Cen. .7C **10**
Slough Town FC .4F **11**
Slough Trad. Est. SL1: Slou .6A **10**
(Ajax Av.)
SL1: Slou .4J **9**
(Banbury Av.)
SL1: Slou .5A **10**
(Liverpool Rd., not continuous)
Smithfield Cl. SL6: Maide .2A **12**
Smithfield Rd. SL6: Maide .2A **12**
Smith's La. SL4: Wind .1H **21**
Snape Spur SL1: Slou .5D **10**
Snowball Hill SL6: Maide .3B **12**
(not continuous)
Snowden Cl. SL4: Wind .3G **21**
Somerford Cl. SL6: Maide .4J **7**
Somersby Cres. SL6: Maide .2F **13**
Somerset Way SL0: Rich P .1G **19**
Somerville Rd. SL4: Eton .4B **16**
Sophie Gdns. SL3: L'ly .1J **17**
Sospel Ct. SL2: Farn R .1B **10**
South Av. TW20: Egh .5J **25**
South Cl. SL1: Slou .6G **9**
Southcroft SL2: Slou .3A **10**
TW20: Eng G .4B **24**
Southfield Cl. SL4: Dor .2F **15**
Southfield Gdns. SL1: Burn .4E **8**
Southgate Ho. SL6: Maide .5G **7**
South Grn. SL1: Slou .6D **10**
South Lawn *SL4: Eton .5B 16*
(off South Mdw. La.)
SOUTHLEA .1G **23**
Southlea Rd. SL3: Dat .7G **17**
SL4: Wind .3F **23**
South Mdw. La. SL4: Eton .5B **16**
South Path SL4: Wind .7B **16**
South Rd. SL6: Maide .6F **7**
TW20: Eng G .5C **24**
South Ter. SL4: Wind .7D **16**
South Vw. SL4: Eton, Eton W .4A **16**
Southwold Spur SL3: L'ly .1D **18**
Sovereign Beeches
SL2: Farn C .5D **4**
Sovereign Hgts. SL3: Dat .5B **18**
Spackmans Way SL1: Slou .2B **16**
Speedbird Way UB7: Harm .6J **19**
Spencer Gdns. TW20: Eng G .4D **24**
Spencer Rd. SL3: L'ly .2A **18**
Spencers Cl. SL6: Maide .4E **6**
Spencers Rd. SL6: Maide .4E **6**
Spens SL6: Maide .4G **7**
Sperling Rd. SL6: Maide .3G **7**
Spinners Wlk. SL4: Wind .7B **16**
Spinney SL1: Slou .7A **10**
Spinney La. SL4: Wink .7E **20**
SPITAL .2A **22**
Spitfire Cl. SL3: L'ly .3B **18**
Springate Fld. SL3: L'ly .1K **17**
Spring Av. TW20: Egh .5E **24**
Spring Cl. SL6: Maide .2G **7**
Springfield SL1: Slou .2G **17**
Springfield Cl. SL4: Wind .1A **22**
Springfield Pk. SL6: Holy .4J **13**
Springfield Rd. SL3: L'ly .6C **18**
SL4: Wind .1A **22**
Spring Hill SL6: Maide .2F **13**
Spring La. SL1: Slou .7J **9**
SL2: Farn R .6D **4**
Spring Ri. TW20: Egh .5E **24**
Spruce Ct. SL1: Slou .2E **16**
Spur, The SL1: Slou .4G **9**
Spur Dr. SL1: Slou .4D **10**
Square, The UB7: Lford .7J **19**
Squirrel Dr. SL4: Wink .7E **20**
Squirrel La. SL4: Wink .7E **20**
Stafferton Way SL6: Maide .6G **7**
Stafford Av. SL2: Slou .3B **10**
Stafford Cl. SL6: Tap .5E **8**
Stag Meadow .3A **22**
Staines Bri. TW18: Staines .4K **25**
Staines By-Pass TW19: Staines .1J **25**
Staines Rd. TW19: Wray .6K **23** & 1F **25**
Stamford Rd. SL6: Maide .6D **6**
Stanhope Rd. SL1: Slou .5G **9**
Stanley Cotts. SL2: Slou .7E **10**
Stanley Grn. E. SL3: L'ly .3A **18**
Stanley Grn. W. SL3: L'ly .3A **18**
Stanton Way SL3: L'ly .3K **17**
Stanwell Moor Rd. UB7: Lford .7J **19**
Starwood Ct. SL3: L'ly .2H **17**
Station App. SL6: Maide .6G **7**
Station Rd. SL1: Slou .5H **9**
SL3: L'ly .2B **18**
SL6: Tap .5C **8**
TW19: Wray .5K **23**
TW20: Egh .4G **25**
Station Rd. Nth. TW20: Egh .4G **25**
Staunton Rd. SL2: Slou .4C **10**
Stephen Cl. TW20: Egh .5J **25**
Stephenson Ct. *SL1: Slou .1E 16*
(off Osborne St.)
Stephenson Dr. SL4: Wind .6A **16**
Stevenson Rd. SL2: Hedg .1F **5**
Stewart Av. SL1: Slou .4E **10**
Stewart Cl. SL6: Fifi .7A **14**
Stewart's Dr. SL2: Farn C .3D **4**
Stile Rd. SL3: L'ly .2J **17**
Stirling Cl. SL4: Wind .1G **21**
Stirling Gro. SL6: Maide .4B **6**
Stirling Rd. SL1: Slou .4K **9**
Stockdales Rd. SL4: Eton W .3J **15**
Stockwells SL6: Tap .3A **8**
STOKE COMMON .3J **5**
Stoke Comn. Rd. SL3: Ful .3J **5**
Stoke Ct. Dr. SL2: Stoke P .7G **5**
Stoke Gdns. SL1: Slou .7D **10**
STOKE GREEN .3F **11**
Stoke Grn. SL2: Stoke P .3F **11**
Stoke Pk. .6G **5**
Stoke Pk. Av. SL2: Farn R .2B **10**
STOKE POGES .6J **5**
Stoke Poges La. SL1: Slou .7D **10**
SL2: Slou, Stoke P .5D **10**
Stoke Rd. SL2: Slou, Stoke P .7E **10**
Stokesay SL2: Slou .6E **10**
Stoke Vw. SL1: Slou .7E **10**
Stoke Wood SL2: Stoke P .3H **5**
Stompits Rd. SL6: Holy .5J **13**
Stomp Rd. SL1: Burn .4E **8**
Stonebridge Fld. SL4: Eton .4A **16**
Stonefield Pk. SL6: Maide .5D **6**
Stoneylands Ct. TW20: Egh .4F **25**
Stoneylands Rd. TW20: Egh .4F **25**
Stoney La. SL2: Farn R .7C **4**
Stoney Meade SL1: Slou .7A **10**
Stornaway Rd. SL3: L'ly .3D **18**
Stour Cl. SL1: Slou .2A **16**
Stovell Rd. SL4: Wind .6A **16**
Stowe Rd. SL1: Slou .6H **9**
Straight Rd. SL4: Old Win .4F **23**
Stranraer Gdns. SL1: Slou .7D **10**
Stratfield Ct. SL6: Maide .4J **7**
Stratfield Rd. SL1: Slou .1F **17**
Stratford Cl. SL2: Slou .3G **9**
Stratford Gdns. SL6: Maide .1D **12**
Streamside SL1: Slou .7J **9**
Strode's Coll. La. *TW20: Egh .4F 25*
(off High St.)
Strode St. TW20: Egh .3G **25**
Stroma Ct. SL1: Slou .6G **9**
Stroud Cl. SL4: Wind .2G **21**
STROUDE .7G **25**
Stroude Rd. GU25: Vir W .7G **25**
TW20: Egh .5G **25**
Stroud Farm Rd. SL6: Holy .5J **13**
Stuart Cl. SL4: Wind .1J **21**
Stuart Way SL4: Wind .1H **21**
STUD GREEN .6F **13**
Sturt Grn. SL6: Holy .5F **13**
Suffolk Cl. SL1: Slou .5H **9**
Suffolk Rd. SL6: Maide .1E **12**
Sumburgh Way SL1: Slou .4D **10**
Summerhouse La. UB7: Harm .5K **19**
Summerlea SL1: Slou .7A **10**
Summerleaze Rd. SL6: Maide .3H **7**
Summers Rd. SL1: Burn .2F **9**
Sunbury Ct. SL4: Eton .5C **16**
Sunbury Rd. SL4: Eton .5C **16**
Sun Cl. SL4: Eton .5C **16**
Sunderland Rd. SL6: Maide .4C **6**
Sun La. SL6: Maide .5F **7**
SUNNYMEADS .3K **23**
Sunnymeads Station (Rail) .2K **23**
Sun Pas. SL4: Wind .7C **16**
Sunray Av. UB7: W Dray .1K **19**
Surly Hall Wlk. SL4: Wind .7J **15**
Surrey Av. SL2: Slou .4B **10**
Sussex Cl. SL1: Slou .1G **17**
Sussex Ho. SL2: Farn C .5E **4**
Sussex Keep SL1: Slou .1G **17**
Sussex Pl. SL1: Slou .1F **17**
(not continuous)
Sutherland Grange SL4: Wind .6G **15**
SUTTON .4D **18**
Sutton Av. SL3: L'ly .1H **17**
Sutton Cl. SL6: Maide .6D **6**
Sutton La. SL3: L'ly .5C **18**
Sutton Pl. SL3: L'ly .5C **18**
Swabey Rd. SL3: L'ly .3B **18**

Swallowfield TW20: Eng G 5B 24
Swanbrook Ct. SL6: Maide 5H 7
Swann Ct. SL1: Slou 2D 16
Swan Ter. SL4: Wind 6A 16
Sweeps La. TW20: Egh 4F 25
Switchback, The SL6: Maide 2E 6
Switchback SL6: Maide 2E 6
Switchback Rd. Nth. SL6: Maide 1F 7
Switchback Rd. Sth. SL6: Maide 2E 6
                          (not continuous)
Sycamore Cl. SL6: Maide 2D 12
Sycamore Ct. SL4: Wind 2B 22
Sycamore Wlk. SL3: G Grn 5K 11
    TW20: Eng G 5B 24
Sydenham Gdns. SL1: Slou 1B 16
Sydney Gro. SL1: Slou 5B 10
Syke Cluan SL0: Rich P 1F 19
Syke Ings SL0: Rich P 2F 19
Sykes Rd. SL1: Slou 5A 10
Sylvester Rd. SL6: Maide 2F 7

T

Talbot Av. SL3: L'ly 1A 18
Talbot Ct. SL4: Wind 2A 22
Talbot Pl. SL3: Dat 7H 17
Talbots Dr. SL6: Maide 6C 6
Tall Trees SL3: Coln 7E 18
Tamarind Ct. TW20: Egh 4F 25
Tamarisk Way SL1: Slou 1K 15
Tamar Way SL3: L'ly 4C 18
Tangier Ct. SL4: Eton 5C 16
Tangier La. SL4: Eton 5C 16
Tapestries Hall SL4: Old Win 4F 23
TAPLOW 3B 8
Taplow Comn. Rd.
    SL1: Burn .1D 8
Taplow Quays SL6: Tap 5K 7
Taplow Rd. SL6: Tap 5D 8
Taplow Station (Rail) 5C 8
Tarbay La. SL4: Oak G 2E 20
Tarmac Way UB7: Harm 6J 19
Tatchbrook Cl. SL6: Maide 4H 7
Tavistock Cl. SL6: Maide 4B 6
Taylor's Bushes Ride
    SL4: Wind 7F 21
Taylors Ct. SL6: Maide 4C 6
Tectonic Pl. SL6: Holy 4J 13
Teesdale Rd. SL2: Slou 4J 9
Telford Dr. SL1: Slou 1K 15
Tempest Rd. TW20: Egh 5J 25
Temple Rd. SL4: Wind 1B 22
Temple Way SL2: Farn C 4E 4
Templewood Ga. SL2: Farn C 4E 4
Templewood La.
    SL2: Farn C, Stoke P 4E 4
Ten Acre La. TW20: Thorpe 7J 25
Tennyson Way SL2: Slou 3H 9
Terrace, The SL6: Bray 2K 13
Terrent Ct. SL4: Wind 7K 15
Testwood Rd. SL4: Wind 7G 15
Thames Av. SL4: Wind 6C 16
Thames Cres. SL6: Maide 2J 7
THAMES HOSPICECARE (WINDSOR)
    . . . . .2K 21
Thames Mead SL4: Wind 7H 15
Thames Rd. SL3: L'ly 3B 18
    SL4: Wind 6F 15
Thames Side SL4: Wind 6C 16
Thames St. SL4: Wind 7C 16
Thames Valley Athletics Cen. 4D 16
Thames Valley University
    Slough Campus 7D 10
Thatchers Dr. SL6: Maide 7B 6
The . . . .
    Names prefixed with 'The' for example
    'The Arches' are indexed under the main
    name such as 'Arches, The'
Theatre Royal
    Windsor 6C 16
Thicket, The SL6: Maide 7A 6

Thicket Gro. SL6: Maide 5A 6
Third Cres. SL6: Maide 4B 10
Thirkleby Cl. SL1: Slou 7B 10
Thirlmere Av. SL1: Slou 4F 9
Thirlmere Cl. TW20: Egh 6H 25
Thomas Ct. SL6: Maide 3B 12
Thompkins La. SL2: Farn R 6B 4
Thompson Cl. SL3: L'ly 3B 18
Thorncroft TW20: Eng G 6C 24
Thorndike SL2: Slou 4K 9
Thorn Dr. SL3: G Grn 5K 11
THORNEY 2J 19
Thorney Country Pk. 2J 19
Thorney La. Nth. SL0: Iver 1G 19
Thorney La. Sth. SL0: Rich P 1G 19
Thorney Mill Rd. SL0: Thorn 2H 19
                          (not continuous)
    UB7: W Dray 2H 19
Thorpe By-Pass TW20: Thorpe 7H 25
Thorpe Ind. Pk. TW20: Thorpe 7J 25
THORPE LEA 5J 25
Thorpe Lea Rd.
    TW20: Egh, Thorpe 5H 25
Thorpe Rd. TW18: Staines 5K 25
Thrift La. SL6: Holy, Maide 3D 12
                          (not continuous)
Thurlby Way SL6: Maide 2E 12
Thurston Rd. SL1: Slou 5D 10
Tilbury Wlk. SL3: L'ly 2C 18
Tilstone Av. SL4: Eton W 4H 15
Tilstone Cl. SL4: Eton W 4H 15
Timbers Wlk. SL6: Maide 7C 6
Timberwood SL2: Farn C 2F 5
Timbralls SL4: Eton 4C 16
                          (off Slough Rd.)
Tinkers La. SL4: Wind 1G 21
Tinsey Cl. TW20: Egh 4H 25
Tintern Cl. SL1: Slou 2B 16
Tiree Ho. SL2: Slou 3A 10
Tite Hill TW20: Egh, Eng G 4D 24
Tithe Barn Dr. SL6: Bray 4A 14
                          (not continuous)
Tithe Cl. SL6: Holy 4K 13
Tithe Ct. SL3: L'ly 3B 18
TITTLE ROW 7C 6
Tobermory Cl. SL3: L'ly 3K 17
Tockley Rd. SL1: Burn 2E 8
Tollgate SL6: Maide 6B 6
Tomlin Rd. SL2: Slou 3H 9
Topaz Cl. SL1: Slou 7A 10
Torin Ct. TW20: Eng G 4C 24
Torquay Spur SL2: Slou 2A 10
Torridge Rd. SL3: L'ly 5C 18
TOUCHEN END 7E 12
Touchen End Rd. SL6: Holy 7E 12
Tourist Info. Cen.
    Maidenhead 5H 7
    Windsor 7C 16
Tower Ho. SL1: Slou 1D 16
Tower Ride SL4: Wind 7H 21
Town & Crown Exhibition 7C 16
Town Sq. SL1: Slou 1E 16
Tozer Wlk. SL4: Wind 2G 21
Tracy Av. SL3: L'ly 4A 18
Travic Rd. SL2: Slou 2J 9
Travis Ct. SL2: Farn R 2A 10
Treesmill Dr. SL6: Maide 2C 12
Trelawney Av. SL3: L'ly 2J 17
Trenchard Rd. SL6: Holy 5J 13
Trenches La. SL3: L'ly 1B 18
Trent Rd. SL3: L'ly 5C 18
Trent Vs. SL3: Dat 7G 17
                          (off Datchet Pl.)
Tressel, The SL6: Maide 6E 6
Trevelyan Ct. SL4: Wind 1A 22
Trevose Ho. SL2: Slou 3A 10
                          (off Franklin Av.)
Trinity Pl. SL4: Wind 1B 22
Troutbeck Cl. SL2: Slou 6F 11
Trumper Way SL1: Slou 7J 9
Truro Cl. SL6: Maide 5B 6
Tubwell Rd. SL2: Stoke P 7K 5

Tudor Ct. SL6: Maide 2K 7
    TW20: Egh 4G 25
Tudor Gdns. SL1: Slou 5F 9
Tudor La. SL4: Old Win 6H 23
Tudor Way SL4: Wind 7H 15
Tulip Way UB7: W Dray 3K 19
Tuns La. SL1: Slou 2B 16
Turks Head Ct. SL4: Eton 6C 16
Turner Rd. SL3: L'ly 1H 17
Turnoak Pk. SL4: Wind 3H 21
Turpins Grn. SL6: Maide 7B 6
Turton Way SL1: Slou 2C 16
Tweed Rd. SL3: L'ly 5C 18
Twinches La. SL1: Slou 7A 10
Two Mile Dr. SL1: Slou 1H 15
Twynham Rd. SL6: Maide 5C 6
Tyle Pl. SL4: Old Win 4F 23
Tyler Wlk. SL3: L'ly 4A 18
Tynedale M. SL1: Slou 1A 16
Tyrell Gdns. SL4: Wind 2J 21

U

Ullswater Cl. SL1: Slou 4F 9
Umberville Way SL2: Slou 2J 9
Underhill Cl. SL6: Maide 6F 7
Upcroft SL4: Wind 2A 22
Up. Bray Rd. SL6: Bray 3K 13
Up. Lees Rd. SL2: Slou 2A 10
UPTON 2F 17
Upton Cl. SL1: Slou 2E 16
Upton Ct. Rd. SL3: L'ly, Slou 2F 17
UPTON HOSPITAL 1E 16
Upton Lea Pde. SL2: Slou 6G 11
UPTON PARK 2E 16
Upton Pk. SL1: Slou 2D 16
Upton Rd. SL1: Slou 2F 17
Uxbridge Rd. SL1: Slou 1F 17
    SL2: Slou .1G 17
    SL3: G Grn, Wex 4K 11

V

Vale Gro. SL1: Slou 2D 16
Vale Rd. SL4: Wind 6J 15
Valley End SL3: Wex 3H 11
Vansittart Est. SL4: Wind 6B 16
Vansittart Rd. SL4: Wind 7A 16
Vantage Rd. SL1: Slou 7A 10
Vanwall Bus. Pk.
    SL6: Maide 7D 6
Vanwall Rd. SL6: Maide 1C 12
Vaughan Copse SL4: Eton 3C 16
Vaughan Gdns. SL4: Eton W 3J 15
Vaughan Way SL2: Slou 3H 9
Vauxhall Rd. SL6: Maide 1D 12
Vegal Cres. TW20: Eng G 4B 24
Venus Cl. SL2: Slou 3J 9
Verbena Cl. UB7: W Dray 4K 19
Verdon Ct. SL2: Farn R 2A 10
Vermont Rd. SL2: Slou 3J 9
Verney Rd. SL3: L'ly 3B 18
Vicarage Av. TW20: Egh 4H 25
Vicarage Cl. TW20: Egh 5H 25
Vicarage Cres. TW20: Egh 4H 25
Vicarage Dr. SL6: Bray 1K 13
Vicarage Gdns. SL6: W Walt 5A 12
Vicarage La. TW19: Wray 7K 23
    TW18: Staines 2K 25
    TW20: Egh 4G 25
Vicarage Wlk. SL6: Bray 1K 13
Vicarage Way SL3: Coln 6D 18
Victor Cl. SL6: Maide 4C 6
Victoria Ct. SL1: Slou 7D 10
                          (off Blair Rd.)
Victoria Dr.
    SL1: Burn, Farn C 5A 4
    SL2: Farn C 5A 4
Victoria M. TW20: Eng G 5C 24

Victoria Rd. SL2: Farn C 5E 4
   SL2: Slou .7G 11
   SL4: Eton W 3H 15
Victoria St. SL1: Slou 1E 16
   SL4: Wind 7C 16
   TW20: Eng G 5C 24
Victor Rd. SL4: Wind 2B 22
Village Rd. SL4: Dor 2E 14
Village Shop. Cen. SL1: Slou 1E 16
   (off Buckingham Gdns.)
Villiers Ct. SL4: Wind 6K 15
Villiers Ho. SL4: Eton 4B 16
   (off Common La.)
Villiers Rd. SL2: Slou 4C 10
Vine Rd. SL2: Stoke P 5H 5
Viscount Ct. SL4: Wind 7B 16

W

Wade Dr. SL1: Slou 7K 9
Wagner Cl. SL6: Maide 2A 12
Wakefield Cres. SL2: Stoke P 5H 5
Waldeck Rd. SL6: Maide 5H 7
Walk, The SL4: Eton W 4K 15
Walker Ct. SL6: Maide 5E 6
Walker Cres. SL3: L'ly 4A 18
Walker Rd. SL6: Bray 1H 13
Wallace Wlk. SL4: Eton 4E 16
Wallis Ct. SL1: Slou 1F 17
Walnut Lodge SL1: Slou 2C 16
Walpole Ho. SL4: Eton 5B 16
   (off Eton Wick Rd.)
Walpole Rd. SL1: Slou 5G 9
   SL4: Old Win 6G 23
Waltham Cl. SL6: Maide 3A 12
Waltham Rd. SL6: W Walt 5A 12
Walton La. SL2: Farn C 1J 9
Wapshott Rd. TW18: Staines 5K 25
Ward Gdns. SL1: Slou 6H 9
Ward Royal SL4: Wind 7B 16
Ward Royal Pde. SL4: Wind 7B 16
   (off Alma Rd.)
Ward's Pl. TW20: Egh 5J 25
Warner Cl. SL1: Slou 7H 9
Warre Ho. SL4: Eton 4B 16
   (off Common La.)
Warren Cl. SL3: L'ly 2K 17
Warren Ct. SL2: Farn C 4E 4
Warren Pde. SL2: Slou 7H 11
Warrington Av. SL1: Slou 5B 10
Warrington Spur SL4: Old Win 6G 23
Warwick Av. SL2: Slou 3B 10
   TW20: Egh 7J 25
Warwick Cl. SL6: Maide 2C 12
Warwick Ct. SL4: Wind 1B 22
   (off Alma Rd.)
Warwick Vs. TW20: Egh 7J 25
Washington Dr. SL1: Slou 2H 9
   SL4: Wind 2H 21
Waterbeach Cl. SL1: Slou 5C 10
Waterbeach Rd. SL1: Slou 5C 10
Waterford Ho. UB7: W Dray 2K 19
Waterman Ct. SL1: Slou 7H 9
Watermans Bus. Pk.
   TW18: Staines 3K 25
WATER OAKLEY 5C 14
Water Oakley Farm SL4: Wat O 5C 14
Waterside UB7: Harm 6K 19
Waterside Dr. SL3: L'ly 1A 18
Waters Reach SL6: Maide 3H 7
Wavell Gdns. SL2: Slou 2J 9
Wavell Rd. SL6: Maide 6C 6
Wavendene Av. TW20: Egh 6H 25
Waverley Rd. SL1: Slou 4B 10
Waylands TW19: Wray 5K 23
Waynflete SL4: Eton 5B 16
   (off Common La.)
Wayside M. SL6: Maide 4G 7
Webb Cl. SL3: L'ly 3J 17
Webster Cl. SL6: Maide 7B 6
Weekes Dr. SL1: Slou 7A 10

Weint, The SL3: Coln 6D 18
Weirside Gdns. UB7: W Dray 1K 19
Welbeck Rd. SL6: Maide 7E 6
Welby Cl. SL6: Maide 1B 12
Welden St. SL2: Slou 5H 11
Welland Cl. SL3: L'ly 5C 18
Wellbank SL6: Tap 3B 8
Wellcroft Rd. SL1: Slou 7A 10
Wellesley Av. SL0: Rich P 2G 19
Wellesley Ct. SL0: Rich P 1G 19
Wellesley Ho. SL4: Wind 7A 16
   (off Vansittart Rd.)
Wellesley Path SL1: Slou 1F 17
   (off Wellesley Rd.)
Wellesley Rd. SL1: Slou 7F 11
Welley Av. TW19: Wray 3K 23
Welley Rd. SL3: Hort 5K 23
   TW19: Wray 5K 23
Wellhouse Rd. SL6: Maide 2F 7
Wellington Cl. SL6: Maide 4C 6
Wellington Lodge SL4: Wink 7E 20
Wellington Rd. SL6: Maide 5E 6
Wellington St. SL1: Slou 7D 10
Wells Cl. SL4: Wind 7K 15
Wendover Pl. TW18: Staines 4K 25
Wendover Rd. SL1: Burn 4E 8
   TW18: Staines 4J 25
Wentworth Av. SL2: Slou 1K 9
Wentworth Cres. SL6: Maide 6D 6
Wentworth Ind. Ct. SL2: Slou 2J 9
Wesley Dr. TW20: Egh 5G 25
Wesley Pl. SL4: Wink 7E 20
Wessex Way SL6: Maide 1C 12
Westacott Bus. Cen.
   SL6: L Grn 3A 12
Westborough Ct. SL6: Maide 6D 6
Westborough Rd. SL6: Maide 6D 6
Westbrook SL6: Bray 4B 14
Westbury SL4: Eton 5B 16
   (off Eton Wick Rd.)
West Ct. SL6: Bray 1K 13
West Cres. SL4: Wind 7J 15
Westcroft SL2: Slou 3A 10
West Dean SL6: Maide 4G 7
WEST DRAYTON 1K 19
West End Ct. SL2: Stoke P 7H 5
West End La. SL2: Stoke P 7G 5
Western Perimeter Rd.
   TW6: H'row A 7J 19
   UB7: Lford 7J 19
Westfield La. SL3: G Grn 5J 11
Westfield Rd. SL2: Slou 3A 10
   SL6: Maide 5C 6
Westgate Cres. SL1: Slou 6J 9
Westgate Retail Pk. SL1: Slou 6K 9
Westlands Av. SL1: Slou 5F 9
Westlands Cl. SL1: Slou 5F 9
Westmead SL4: Wind 2A 22
   SL6: Maide 2G 7
Westmorland Rd. SL6: Maide 5E 6
Weston Rd. SL1: Slou 4J 9
Westons Yd. SL4: Eton 5C 16
West Point SL1: Slou 7G 9
West Rd. SL6: Maide 5F 7
West St. SL6: Maide 5G 7
Wethered Dr. SL1: Burn 4E 8
Wetton Pl. TW20: Egh 4F 25
Wexford Ct. SL6: Maide 5J 7
WEXHAM 3G 11
WEXHAM COURT 5H 11
WEXHAM PARK HOSPITAL 3H 11
Wexham Pk. Stadium 5F 11
Wexham Pk. La. SL3: Wex 3H 11
Wexham Rd. SL1: Slou 1F 17
   SL2: Slou, Wex 5G 11
Wexham Sports Cen. 1G 11
WEXHAM STREET 1H 11
Wexham St. SL2: Stoke P, Wex 3G 11
   SL3: Stoke P, Wex 3G 11
Wexham Woods SL3: Wex 4H 11
Wharf Rd. TW19: Wray 6H 23
Wheatbutts, The SL4: Eton W 3J 15

Wheatfield Cl. SL6: Maide 1B 12
Wheatlands Rd. SL3: Slou 2G 17
Wheatsheaf Pde. SL4: Old Win 4F 23
   (off St Luke's Rd.)
Wheatstone Cl. SL3: Slou 2F 17
Wheelwrights Pl. SL3: Coln 6D 18
Whitby Rd. SL1: Slou 6B 10
Whitby Rd. Bus. Cen.
   SL1: Slou 6B 10
Whitchurch Cl. SL6: Maide 1F 7
Whiteacres Dr. SL6: Holy 4J 13
Whitebrook Pk. SL6: Maide 1K 7
White Cl. SL1: Slou 7C 10
Whiteford Rd. SL2: Slou 4D 10
Whitehall Farm La.
   GU25: Vir W 7E 24
   (not continuous)
Whitehall La. TW20: Egh 6F 25
White Hart Rd. SL1: Slou 2C 16
Whitehart Rd. SL6: Maide 5G 7
Whitehaven SL1: Slou 6E 10
White Hermitage SL4: Old Win 4H 23
White Horse Rd. SL4: Wind 2G 21
Whitehouse Way SL3: L'ly 2J 17
Whiteley SL4: Wind 6H 15
White Lillies Island SL4: Wind 6K 15
White Paddock SL6: Maide 3B 12
White Rock SL6: Maide 3J 7
Whites La. SL3: Dat 5G 17
WHITE WALTHAM 5A 12
Whittaker Rd. SL2: Slou 3G 9
Whittenham Cl. SL2: Slou 7F 11
Whittle Parkway SL1: Slou 5G 9
Wickets, The SL6: Maide 5D 6
Wickham La. TW20: Egh 6G 25
Wick La. TW20: Eng G 5A 24
Wick Rd. TW20: Eng G 7A 24
Widbrook Rd. SL6: Maide 1J 7
Wiggington Ho. SL4: Eton 6C 16
   (off High St.)
Wilberforce M. SL6: Maide 5G 7
   (off St Luke's Rd.)
Wild Grn. Nth. SL3: L'ly 3B 18
Wild Grn. Sth. SL3: L'ly 3B 18
Wilford Rd. SL3: L'ly 3K 17
Willant Cl. SL6: Maide 3A 12
William Ellis Cl. SL4: Old Win 4F 23
William Hartley Yd. SL3: Wex 3G 11
Williams Hall TW20: Eng G 2C 24
   (off Coopers Hill La.)
William St. SL1: Slou 1E 16
   SL4: Wind 7C 16
Willoners SL2: Slou 4K 9
Willoughby Rd. SL3: L'ly 2B 18
Willowbrook SL4: Eton 3C 16
Willow Cl. SL3: Coln 6D 18
Willow Dr. SL6: Holy 3J 13
Willow Pde. SL3: L'ly 2B 18
Willow Pk. SL2: Stoke P 6J 5
Willow Pl. SL4: Eton 5B 16
Willows, The SL4: Wind 6G 15
Willows Lodge SL4: Wind 6G 15
Willows Path SL4: Wind 7F 15
Willows Riverside Pk.
   SL4: Wind 6F 15
Willow Wlk. TW20: Eng G 4C 24
Willow Wood Cl. SL1: Burn 1E 8
Willson Rd. TW20: Eng G 4B 24
Wilmot Rd. SL1: Burn 2E 8
Wilton Cres. SL4: Wind 3G 21
Wiltshire Av. SL2: Slou 3B 10
Winchester Cl. SL3: Poyle 7F 19
Winchester Dr. SL6: Maide 2C 12
Windermere Cl. TW20: Egh 6H 25
Windermere Way SL1: Slou 4F 9
Windmill Cl. SL4: Wind 1A 22
Windmill Rd. SL1: Slou 7C 10
Windmill Shott TW20: Egh 5F 25
Windrush Av. SL3: L'ly 2C 18
Windrush Way SL6: Maide 4G 7
WINDSOR 7C 16

Windsor & Eton Central Station (Rail)
.................................7C 16
Windsor & Eton FC 3A 22
Windsor & Eton Relief Rd.
  SL4: Eton, Wind 7A 16
Windsor & Eton Riverside Station (Rail)
.................................6C 16
Windsor Boys School Sports Cen. ...7A 16
Windsor Brass Rubbing Cen. 7C 16
  (off High St.)
Windsor Bus. Cen. SL4: Wind 6B 16
Windsor Castle 6D 16
Windsor Cl. SL1: Burn 3F 9
Windsor Fitness & Rackets Club, The
.................................7A 16
Windsor La. SL1: Burn 3F 9
Windsor Leisure Cen. 6A 16
Windsor Rd. SL1: Slou 2D 16
  SL2: Ger X, Stoke P 3J 5
  SL3: Dat 6F 17
  SL4: Old Win 7H 23
  SL4: Wat O, Wind 4A 14
  SL4: Wind 6E 14
  SL6: Bray 2H 13
  SL9: Ger X 1K 5
  TW19: Wray 5K 23
  TW20: Egh 7H 23
Winkfield La. SL4: Wink 7A 20
Winkfield Rd. SL4: Wink 7F 21
Winston Ct. SL6: Maide 4C 6
Winter Hill Rd. SL6: Maide 2B 6
Wintoun Path SL2: Slou 3H 9
Winvale SL1: Slou 2D 16
Winwood SL2: Slou 5H 11
  SL4: Wind 7J 15
Wise La. UB7: W Dray 2K 19

Withey Cl. SL4: Wind 7H 15
Withycroft SL3: G Grn 5K 11
Wolf La. SL4: Wind 2G 21
Wood Cl. SL4: Wind 3B 22
Woodcote SL6: Maide 6E 6
Wood End Cl. SL2: Farn C 2F 5
Woodfield Dr. SL6: Maide 6B 6
Woodford Way SL2: Slou 2K 9
Woodhaw TW20: Egh 3H 25
Woodhurst Nth. SL6: Maide 3K 7
Woodhurst Rd. SL6: Maide 3J 7
Woodhurst Sth. SL6: Maide 3K 7
Woodland Av. SL1: Slou 6C 10
  SL4: Wind 3J 21
Woodland Glade SL2: Farn C 2F 5
Woodland Grange SL0: Rich P 2F 19
Woodlands Bus. Pk.
  SL6: Maide 3B 12
WOODLANDS PARK 3A 12
Woodlands Pk. Av. SL6: Maide 3B 12
Woodlands Pk. Rd. SL6: Maide 3B 12
Wood La. SL1: Slou 2J 15
  SL2: Hedg 1G 5
Woodlee Cl. GU25: Vir W 7C 24
Woods Dr. SL2: Farn C 4B 4
Woodstock Av. SL3: L'ly 3J 17
Woodstock Cl. SL6: Maide 3G 7
WOOLLEY GREEN 7A 6
Wootton Way SL6: Maide 6D 6
Worcester Cl. SL6: Maide 2D 12
Worcester Gdns. SL1: Slou 1C 16
Wordsworth Rd. SL2: Slou 3G 9
Wotton Ho. SL4: Eton 4C 16
  (off Common La.)
WRAYSBURY 5K 23
Wraysbury Lake Sailing Club 4K 23

Wraysbury Rd. TW18: Staines 2J 25
  TW19: Staines 1H 25
Wren Ct. SL3: L'ly 2B 18
Wren Dr. UB7: W Dray 2K 19
Wright SL4: Wind 2F 21
Wright Sq. SL4: Wind 2G 21
Wright Way SL4: Wind 2F 21
  TW6: H'row A 7J 19
  UB7: Lford 7J 19
Wyatt Rd. SL4: Wind 2G 21
Wylands Rd. SL3: L'ly 3B 18
Wymers Cl. SL1: Burn 1E 8
Wymer's Wood Rd. SL1: Burn 1D 8
Wyndham Cres. SL1: Burn 1E 8

Y

Yard Mead TW20: Egh 2G 25
Yarmouth Rd. SL1: Slou 5B 10
Ye Meads SL6: Tap 7B 8
Yeoveney Cl. TW19: Staines 1K 25
Yeovil Ent. Cen. SL2: Slou 4J 9
Yeovil Rd. SL1: Slou 4H 9
Yew Tree Cl. SL6: Maide 4F 7
Yew Tree Rd. SL1: Slou 2F 17
York Av. SL1: Slou 5B 10
  SL4: Wind 1A 22
York Rd. SL4: Wind 1A 22
  SL6: Maide 6G 7

Z

Zetland Ct. SL6: Maide 4J 7